ON BECOMING A ...

REAL
MAN

ON BECOMING A...
REAL MAN

EDWIN LOUIS COLE

THOMAS NELSON PUBLISHERS
Nashville

Published in Nashville, Tennessee, by Thomas Nelson, Inc., and distributed in Canada by Lawson Falle, Ltd., Cambridge, Ontario.

Except where noted otherwise, Scripture quotations are from the NEW KING JAMES VERSION of the Bible. Copyright © 1979, 1980, 1982, Thomas Nelson, Inc., Publishers.

Scripture quotations noted KJV are from the KING JAMES VERSION of the Bible.

Scripture quotations noted NIV are from The Holy Bible: NEW INTERNA-TIONAL VERSION. Copyright © 1978 by the New York International Bible Society. Used by permission of Zondervan Bible Publishers.

Scripture quotations noted LB are from The Living Bible (Wheaton, Illinois: Tyndale House Publishers, 1971) and are used by permission.

Scripture quotations noted AB are from THE AMPLIFIED BIBLE: Old Testament. Copyright © 1962, 1964 by Zondervan Publishing House (used by permission); and from THE AMPLIFIED NEW TESTAMENT. Copyright © 1958 by the Lockman Foundation (used by permission).

Library of Congress Cataloging-in-Publication Data

Cole, Edwin Louis.
    Real man / Edwin Louis Cole.
        p.   cm.
    Includes bibliographical references.
    ISBN 0-8407-7245-9
    1. Men—Conduct of life.   2. Men—Religious life.   3. Jesus
Christ—Example.   I. Title.
BJ1601.C57   1992
248.8'42—dc20   91-45301
                                                    CIP

Printed in the United States of America
1 2 3 4 5 6 7 — 96 95 94 93 92

*To the loveliest lady in the land,
my wife, Nancy Corbett Cole,
who helped me find the Real Man*

Special Thanks . . .

To Paul Cole, whose vision and encouragement made this book possible.

To Joann Webster, without whose tireless effort the manuscript never would have been completed.

To Bruce and Camella Binkley, Jack and Marcella Mackey, MarLynn Feuerstein, Belinda Sikes, and Marti Clark, who assisted me in transcribing, proofing, referencing, and writing. To the entire staff of the Christian Men's Network, whose diligence and effort to fill in the gaps when these others were busy made the work so much easier.

To the supporters and friends of the ministry who encouraged us, supported us financially, offered input, and gave of their lives to see this book completed.

To the many men and women whose identities are obscured on the following pages, but whose courage, heroism, and godliness serve as modern examples for us all.

My deepest gratitude and appreciation to my publisher, Sam Moore, whose encouragement and inspiration, together with his staff, have made this book possible.

Contents

Part 6　Real Roles

Part 1
The Masculinity Maze

■ ■ ■

Chapter 1
The Masculinity Crisis

I love being a man.

I don't feel ashamed, embarrassed, intimidated, or guilty about it. But I know I'm not what I shall be. I am what I am, and I'm more than I was. But I'm not all the man I can be.

Today I know where I'm headed with my masculinity. For years I floundered in my attempts at manhood, never having been taught how to be a man. Through the struggles and difficulties, successes and rewards, I learned much of what being a man really means. Now I can say it's been a wonderful life in many ways. I have a wife I love deeply, children who have matured successfully, a career that— although erratic in some ways—is now a worldwide influence for good and God.

Many people around the world recognize the current crisis in manhood and are trying to correct this basic societal flaw. Let's begin with some basics.

Headlines in the *Boston Globe* newspaper read: "Wanted: Some Stouthearted Men." The article began with the question "What's wrong with America?" and gave this answer: "Lousy leadership. Not just in government or politics, but in business and labor, service and manufacturing, education and other big institutions, and the media, too."[1]

Caustic and critical, but is it true? Most Americans would agree—we have a crisis in leadership and in productivity—but this stems basically from a crisis in manhood. Our manhood has been emasculated, and that has sterilized our ability to reproduce.

The U.S. is not the only country suffering such problems. Hundreds of others have hit a crisis in manhood today head-on; there are scores of problems confronting men in every nation under the sun.

For example, South America's runaway inflation has sapped the vitality of its countries. Even worse, it creates a fatalistic approach to life. Young men feel they have nothing to look forward to and that they are virtually helpless to do anything about the problem. The crisis they are experiencing is not simply economic; it is also a crisis in manhood.

The last time I visited England, statistics published in a major newspaper cited five million people were "on the dole." The article stated that the present generation of youth was without ambition or hope—they were gripped by a welfare mentality.

In Italy, a recent report says that Italian youth admire Mafia members more than government, religious, or industry leaders. Their next preference, after criminal celebrities, is entertainers. The reporter concluded that young people seem to lack any understanding of the normal values that undergird a productive society.

When I was in Germany recently, its citizens told me theirs is a "fatherless nation" because of the monumental loss of men in World War II. For the same reason, Russia is called a "nation without grandfathers." After World War II, only seventeen in a thousand Russians returned from battle, and only three of those seventeen were not wounded or maimed.[2]

In Scotland, male depression runs rampant. In Australia and Central America, the "macho male" mentality has created numerous problems in industry and family relationships. South African men still suffer from apartheid. The Philippines suffer under a matriarchal society that has contributed to a high incidence of homosexuality among men. Reports of Nigerian men flagrantly brutalizing women have created a national concern and international embarrassment. People are motivated by what they *think* is important in this world, whether that perception is true or not. The way the Bible puts it is: "For as he thinks in his heart, so is he" (Prov. 23:7). Perceptions of manhood, gleaned from society's role models—both good and bad—motivate men in behavioral patterns that are positive and negative. These society-dictated perceptions tend to distort true manhood and create confusion.

The feminist movement rails against maleness, creating a new perception of the word *man*. Feminists cry out for the deletion of gender-specific terms and seek to replace them with neuter terms. Gay-rights activists rage against heterosexuality and parade with "I hate straight" banners.

Movies, television, and entertainment give a perception of men as either stupid bunglers or super-macho heroes. Few models of manhood exist anywhere in between. Even "family" television programs show ineffective men depending on competent women to help them through life.

Books and periodicals routinely criticize men for not spending enough time with the family, not doing their fair share of the work at home, not being sensitive to their wives . . . and on the list goes. But when men go to the work place, other standards apply. Men are to behave aggressively: perfecting the art of the deal, making the sale, creating the new project, winning the contract, negotiating to the last penny. They are to compete through any available means—moral or not.

Average men have tried to cope with these conflicting messages by trying to please everyone. They end up castrating their identity, becoming ineffective and sterile males. They hardly please anyone; rather, they become objects of displeasure. No wonder men today are confused about manhood.

In conferences, conventions, and radio and television programs wherever I have ministered to men, one basic question consistently pops up: *What is a real man?*

Is a man to be like the actor, John Wayne, the swaggering, tough icon of old Hollywood's manliness—tall, strong, loyal to friends and a terror to enemies, always standing for right (always knowing what right is!), attractive to women, feared and respected by other men?

Or is a man to be like Alan Alda or Phil Donahue, television's answers to the feminist movement—sympathetic, emotional, sensitive, harmless? Or are men to revert to the idea of a "renaissance man"? Or are men to be like Nelson Mandela, Michael Jackson, Arnold Schwarzenegger, or Nolan Ryan?

What is a real man? What is he like?

Answers spring from every sector—religion, philosophy, mythology, sociology, psychology, pop culture, education, government—everyone has an answer, but not every answer is true. Where, then, should we turn?

The answer to the masculinity crisis is the same answer given for every world crisis from the creation of time: the intervention of Creator God. In the case of male identity and role, the answer is found in God as He revealed Himself on earth in the manhood of Jesus Christ. Through Jesus, God showed us by example how to live as real men here on earth. God revealed to us in physical form what He had already said, that He created man "in His image" and for His purposes. Consequently the essence of real manhood is found not in how a man looks or in what a man does, but in who a man is.

But this leads us to another problem that men have grappled with now for two thousand years. How do we approach this God-man, Jesus Christ? How could we even begin to emulate the deity of a holy God revealed on earth as a man? I admit I still don't have all the answers. But I *have* discovered numerous truths that I now teach around the world, and I *can* tell you that the results of applying these truths border on the incredible.

At one particular meeting, more than two thousand men crowded into an auditorium in Boston. Many of those attending would eventually take the patterns and principles I taught, embrace them, then teach other men, who in turn would teach others, and so the truth spreads. But on that day, as I spoke to those assembled, the revelation of who Jesus really is and what He did for us as men seemed to pierce the minds and hearts of every man there. The weight of truth brought a quiet hush among them which, after several minutes, erupted into an enthusiastic expression of joy. I stopped speaking to give an opportunity for the men who had never committed themselves to "real" manhood to come to the front and publicly make their stand. As hundreds came forward, the others spontaneously began to yell in unison, "Jesus, Jesus, Jesus!"

As they shouted, a conviction set in that was almost palpable. Men who one minute had a perception of manhood gleaned from a lifetime of movies, magazines, and ungodly mentors, suddenly realized that true manhood really meant being like Jesus, the only Man who ever lived exactly as God had created Him to live. Convicted of their lack of manliness, their "wimpiness" in following the crowd, individuals began to rush the stage to throw down vestiges of a man's life gone wrong—drugs, cigarettes, chains, keys to girlfriends' apartments, flasks of alcohol, lottery tickets, brass knuckles. In about fifteen minutes, the stage was littered with the symbols of worldly manhood. Then the noise died down and the men began to sing. What a sound! It was as if the top had been lifted off that building and the sounds of a heavenly choir of male voices were wafting down from the corridors of heaven.

There were no drums to beat, no secluded places to go, but right there in the heart of Boston, right in the heart of Urban USA, men were set free. Free to be men!

There is no greater joy or fulfillment for any man than to be brought up to the level of Christlike manhood—"real" manhood.

This was just one day in those men's lives. What would they do from there? I know from experience, and from the hundreds of letters I receive, that men who grasp what real manhood is and begin to walk in that awareness—committing themselves to becoming real men each day—see a consistent, dramatic change in their lives from the very moment of their commitment.

Real manhood cannot be found in just a moment's emotional outburst. Neither is real manhood found in the image of physical prowess and handsomeness. Nor in personality, talent, intelligence, performance, or profession. Real manhood is found within the heart of a man, the "inner man," his moral character, the "real man" that exudes beyond all external devices for the rest of the world to see.

Men cannot mature in moral distinctiveness with mere "head knowledge" or an "emotional catharsis," but we must constantly be evolving, purifying, changing the inmost parts of our being. These inward elements create true quality in every part of life—not the exterior of a product, but the interior; not the polish on a chrome bumper, but the smooth purr of a well-tuned engine; not the talent on a ball field, but the citizenship and integrity when the spotlights go out. The quality of the inner man makes a man "real."

I was pastoring a church in San Bruno, California, just after World War II, when I began to learn what a real man is. Babies were "booming," former soldiers resumed their careers, suburbs sprang up, and congregations rapidly built and enlarged churches to accommodate everyone.

When Nancy and I accepted the church's call to ministry, only the unfinished shell of a building stood on the property. There were bare walls, a concrete floor, and old wooden benches inside. We tried to remodel the building with volunteer labor, small amounts of cash, and donated or used materials. Most of the volunteers were just that—they had little or no experience in the construction business, but wanted to give their time. Scientists painted wood trim, teachers laid tile, preachers moved scaffolding, homemakers nailed plywood. . . . Everybody worked hard.

We did have a few genuine craftsmen, however. One of them was Paul, a contractor, carpenter, and a craftsman of the highest degree. His woodwork was in great demand in San Francisco. During the week he built high-quality (and high-priced!) houses, but he spent his Saturdays helping us complete our building.

Paul's final task was to put a wooden veneer on the wall directly behind the sanctuary's pulpit. As he labored the rest of us were awed by the difference his exquisite work made in our building. We were proud—thrilled—that he had come to help us, and eager to tell everyone of his accomplishments. So it came as a shock when, the day Paul finished, he took me aside and asked me not to tell anyone he had done the woodwork.

"Paul, why?" I asked. "You have worked so hard and done such a beautiful thing for us! I want to tell everyone what a great job you've done."

"Please don't," he reiterated. "I'll show you why."

He proceeded to show me where the wood grain did not match exactly, where the miter was not perfectly joined, and the levels were off a fraction of an inch—things I would never have noticed if he had not pointed them out.

"I was glad to help," he said. "However, this work is not really up

to my standard and I would rather not have people know I did it."
Then he hit me with it.

"I could have done a better job if the material we used had been of better quality."

I never forgot that lesson: *The quality of the product depends on the quality of the material used.*

Its corollary is equally true: *The cheaper the merchandise, the higher the gloss.* When the quality of the material is inferior, high gloss is necessary to camouflage the real product.

Furniture, made from quality wood, generally has only some polish to burnish it and bring out the excellence of the piece. However, furniture made from inferior woods generally has layers of lacquer or paint applied to give it a gloss that conceals the poor quality.

Knives made of tempered steel and a bone handle usually have nothing but a stamp on the blade designating the temper of the steel, and the bone is used in its natural state. However, knives made of plastic and pot metal most often have chrome on the blade, and paint on the handle to give them a gloss that hides the cheap quality. The cheaper the merchandise, the higher the gloss.

True of furniture.

True of knives.

True of women . . .

Prostitutes adorn themselves with flashy external accoutrements to hide the cheapness of their character. They put on layers of paint, clothing, cars, jewelry—high gloss for cheap merchandise.

. . . And true of men.

Con artists, whether in the ghetto or the executive board room, are slick and sophisticated, trying to impress people with outward show to disguise their fraudulent practices.

A man of cheap character always tries to associate with, gain identity from, or control people of great talent or character. He vicariously draws upon others' identities to compensate for his own lack of integrity. Whatever he has is by association with others. Since his name is untrustworthy, he is always a name-dropper.

By contrast, the quality of the material used in becoming a "real man" results in high quality. A real man's strength of character can be relied upon. He doesn't defraud others for money, recognition, or even the respect of his family. He is real in every area of life, in every facet of his being.

Every man is limited in life by three things:

(1) the knowledge in his mind;
(2) the worth of his character; and
(3) the principles upon which he builds his life.[3]

These things shape a man within, for better or worse. They define the quality of his life. Quality is always internal, not external.

The quality of a nation depends on the moral character of its people and the principles upon which they build their individual lives. The truth of this shines clearly in the history of Israel. They had a crisis in leadership and manhood that parallels ours today.

During the period of the judges, Gideon led Israel for a season. He died, leaving seventy sons. One was named Jotham (Judges 9:7–15). Governmental leaders crowned Jotham's half-brother, Abimelech, king and allowed him to kill all his brothers to secure the kingdom. Only Jotham escaped. After the massacre, Jotham stood at a safe distance and called out the Parable of the Bramble Bush as an indictment against them. In the parable, the olive, fig, and grapevine all refused to become king of the trees because they were content with their private lives. So the trees asked the bramble bush to be king. The bramble accepted, but with arrogant demands that far exceeded its worth, saying the other trees must humble themselves and bow down beneath it or else fire would come out of it to destroy them.

Jotham used the parable to prophesy how Abimelech and his aides, who were to be the nation's leaders, would become enemies because they lacked the qualities necessary to lead. This story illustrates how qualified would-be leaders refuse public service because they are content with, and want to retain, their wealth and positions. Even today we find high-caliber men who won't serve in public office. Therefore, vain, ambitious men fill the leadership vacuum and arrogantly demand too much from the people they should serve. The "Bramble Bush" problem has existed in every society, including ours.

In the U.S., some leaders cavort drunkenly in public, are indicted for illicit or immoral acts, accused of fraud and mismanagement, and yet say it is none of the public's business how they conduct themselves in private. The truth is, whatever a man is in private—what he believes, practices, and has built into his character—determines the actions and decisions he makes in public. Not just politicians, but some ministers need to correct the same erroneous thinking.

Private philosophy determines public performance.

Not every man with character and integrity has the calling or capacity to serve in public office, but those who do must carefully consider the need, instead of flippantly dismissing the idea. The world depends on them.

One of the wisest men I ever met taught me a great lesson about the importance of building good character. When I was a young man just starting out in ministry, Rev. W. T. Gaston, a greatly admired senior clergyman, came to help me in a visit to a wealthy woman. We were told she may be inclined to give a sizable offering toward a charity we worked with.

We met the rich, obese woman, sitting in a rocking chair in the living room of her comfortable home, surrounded by her many cats, who had the run of the place. In talking with her we realized she was living a miserly existence, consumed with personal concern for her money and cats, had no intention of giving to a charity, and she let us know in no uncertain terms that her money was to be a legacy to her cats.

"What did you make of that?" I asked as we quickly drove away.

"Well, son," my clergy friend answered, "when the charm wears off you have nothing but character left."

Charm is for the instant; character will last.

Charm deals with the external, character with the internal. Charming manners that disguise a poor character will one day vanish, revealing the truth underneath.

THE IMAGE LIE

One problem contributing to the crisis in men today is the reward system offered for presenting a great exterior. Today's cultural psychology advises: Present yourself well, and you'll be rewarded, regardless of your character (at least for a while).

The "problem" professional athletes of today promenaded through their colleges, being lauded, compensated, and rewarded for their talent, not their personhood. Once into the high-pressured world of professional sports, they do not have the necessary inner strength to withstand the adversities, pressures, and temptations confronting them. They use drugs, alcohol, gambling, violence, and sex for escape, comfort, nurture, and relief from tensions and anxieties. Many end up addicted and some even expelled from the sport they love. By contrast, some of the great athletes of all time we remember because of their great charity, citizenship, and integrity.

Fame can come in a moment, but greatness comes with longevity. I spoke on this topic at a National Football League team chapel. The head coach quoted it to the press the next day, and his quotation went out on the Associated Press wire service. A year later, a sportscaster repeated it on television. They remember it and repeat it because they recognize its validity in the sports world. It's true in every way. Greatness comes over the course of time. Those becoming real men build not on what they can gain from the moment, but on what will benefit for life. Life is composed of our choices, constructed by our words, and revealed by our character.

Consider Abraham and Lot (Gen. 13). When God called Abraham out from Ur of the Chaldees, Abraham took along his nephew Lot, and they traveled to a new land. Standing on a hillside and looking across a valley, Abraham gave Lot first choice of where he wanted to live. Lot looked at the well-watered verdant orchards and the alabaster-white houses in the valley before him and chose it over the rock-strewn mountains. But behind those alabaster white walls, and lying in the midst of those lush fields, lay the already wicked cities of Sodom and Gomorrah.

Abraham chose what Lot rejected, the terrain of Canaan with all its unproven but promised worth and value. Years later, when Abraham was prospering and Lot had moved inside the city limits of Sodom, Abraham had to rescue Lot and intercede with God to send angels to rescue Lot again just before the destruction of Sodom and Gomorrah.

Lot's pivotal choice sprang from his day-to-day decisions. The Bible recounts that everywhere Abraham went he "pitched his tents," and "built his altars." He concentrated on the permanent issues of life, constructed his character, and developed a lasting relationship with God. He understood the transient status of life. Lot, however, built an altar only after irreparable harm had come to him and his family.

In a perverted society, men "pitch" their altars and "build" their tents. In other words, they "pitch" their character and "build" their personality. Wrong strategy. Poor results.

Build your character on the foundation of truth, use faithfulness as its cornerstone, make righteousness its walls, and your good character will be known by all; it will stand the test of time. Those are characteristics of Jesus Christ, our model of "real" manhood. To try to develop a godly character apart from God will fail; developing Christlikeness from a heart turned toward God will cause a man to stand for all eternity. God alone makes this so. We go as far as we can in ourselves, but ultimately God must make up the difference for us—this is why Jesus had to die for our sins, for we could not compensate for our own lack of godliness. Jesus said while on earth that only God was "good," and that He did only those things God told Him to do. We should study Jesus' character and attributes to discover how to become "real men," the men God created us to be. More than putting on a veneer of Christlike manhood, Jesus' character and attributes must be rooted deep within us, so we can grow in our relationship with Him.

Becoming a real man requires an ongoing, purifying change in the inmost parts of a man's being. Only God knows the hearts of men. We can depend on Him to reveal our hearts to us, to do a purifying work within us, and cause us to become Christlike—"real men."

Knowing that we live in a world that tries to find other ways to accomplish life's superior purposes with inferior ways, we need to reject substitutes and contend with things that are real.

Chapter 2
The Substitute Society

Two years ago my wife, Nancy, and I spent a delightful week in Vienna, Austria, just before Christmas. We saw the great statues of national heroes, massive ancient buildings abutting the street with their frescoes and pilasters, holiday-decked streets and roadways winding around the magnificent Blue Danube. The Christmas lights lit up amid celebration and song. Christmas left no corner of the city untouched.

And yet, one thing was missing—Jesus—the cause of the celebration. The people had lost the very reason for the festivity itself! Santa Claus was heralded as the substitute for the Christ. In the forty-two years since my eyes opened to the reality of Jesus, this human blindness still amazes me.

So much of our world is deceived the same way. Christmas isn't the only time we are a "substitute society."

Artificial sweetener, artificial insemination, sperm banks, hamburger helper; surrogate mothers, fathers, and sex partners; even the holiday decorations we enjoy each year, are all part of the substitute society we live in. We substitute cubic zirconium for diamonds, vinyl for leather, synthetics for silk, plastic for wood, the counterfeit for the real. Substance is replaced by things of similar, but often inferior, quality. A fast-growing trend in plastic surgery today is "muscle implants" for people who don't (won't?) exercise.

Some substitutes are valid and necessary, others are dangerous and ruinous. Substituting relative values for absolutes in moral life can be devastating.

Some historians call us a "plastic people." Ecologists scream for attention to what they call a "throwaway" society. We often throw away people and keep things. The word *value* itself has lost its meaning.

WHAT EXACTLY ARE VALUES?

During the 1960s a group of social scientists developed a teaching method called "Values Clarification," the process of determining what may or may not be right for a person in any given situation. On this scenario, all moral "oughts" are reduced from universal, absolute values to individual, relative values. What's right for me may not be right for you, but that's okay. The social scientists claimed it was a way to teach values to school-aged children without taking any specific moral position. The basic philosophy behind the teaching is that no absolute values exist, or, as its proponents put it, values are "personal things."

Dr. Sidney Simon and Merrill Harmin taught educators that it was wrong to instruct children that murder and stealing are bad. Teaching that honesty and loyalty are good was equally wrong. They said the teacher should do no more than help the student clarify his own values. Mr. Baer, an associate professor at New York State College wrote in the *Wall Street Journal* that "values clarification" in essence gave the message to adolescents that parents, the school, or society had no right to tell them what standards should guide their behavior, especially sexually. Such a philosophy is akin to giving a knife and fork to a cannibal to help him to a better life.

Bill Murray—son of the infamous atheist Madelyn Murray O'Hare who fought, and won, against school prayer in the U.S.—wrote a tract on "values clarification." After being dragged unwillingly through courtrooms during his school days, Bill now fights to undo what his mother did to public schools. Murray concludes, "We must return moral instruction to our schools. Absolute right and absolute wrong do exist."[1]

Society has substituted relativism for absolutes and has perverted our values. The values of our society are reflected in "our heroes, what we spend our money on, what we watch on TV," according to *Newsweek* journalist Nicols Fox. She points out,

> It's not so much that [the church's] moral leadership is being ignored as that, to a great extent, they've abdicated the role. Collectively, they seem to exude the same relativism and insecurity about right and wrong as the rest of us.[2]

She concludes that the society as a whole has been left yearning for absolutes.

Columnist William Murchison points out that the Protestant work ethic is "on its last legs." At one time, we believed in "hard work, paying debts, staying married, obeying our parents, and going to church." But according to Murchison, today people say,

> "Yuk! So early twentieth century!" . . . And so successful in nurturing the habits that bound families together, that kept the streets safe, that engendered trust, responsibility and social peace. Were the old days better than the new days? Of course they were! Not perfect; just better.[3]

A recent survey of more than seven hundred British youth, ages seventeen to twenty-four, revealed that they valued conformity above rebellion. Shocked researchers found that the average respondent spent nearly six hours a week in bars and used one-fifth of his or her weekly income while there. "For young men, drinking and getting drunk is an important social ritual."[4] They conform to the values they hold.

The practice of substitution leads to perverted philosophies and practices that display blatant inconsistencies. Many of those caught up in our substitute society claim that bad is good and good is bad (Isa. 5:20; Prov. 17:15), deceiving themselves into living a lie rather than embracing truth (Ps. 52:1–4). In doing so they try to justify their inconsistencies.

Today most self-avowed humanists oppose the death penalty for murder, but fight for the right to murder unborn children. How inconsistent! Letting the guilty go free, but destroying the innocent.

It's easier for some to try to make God in their image, rather than conforming themselves to His image (Rom. 1:21–24; 8:29). For instance, the New Age movement proliferates in churches that worship a god of their own making, rather than submit to the leadership of Christ. Such cults demand that God conform to their life-style rather than making their life-styles conform to God's Word.

It's easier to bring homosexuality out of the closet than to clean the closet. Interesting, isn't it? While the secularists "come out of the closet," they want to push Christians into one. In 1988, Tim Robertson wrote,

Many today are following an agenda that Lenin spoke of decades ago when he said he would not speak of being an atheist, but rather would speak of religion as being an entirely private matter. His strategy was to promote the concept that people are free to express religion if done so in a purely private matter. To many people, this sounds harmless enough, but the net effect, however, is to strip Christianity from the public arena.

Liberal members of Congress and the secular media are now combining in an effort to force Christianity into the realm of "private expression."[5]

Intellectuals, whose work changed the philosophies that undergird our society, displayed incredible inconsistencies in their own lives. Karl Marx, the self-professed liberator of humanity, used racist slurs against a political opponent and altered the true findings of his research on *Das Kapital* to make it fit his thesis.[6] Jean Jacques Rousseau, whose *Social Contract* promoted more justice in politics and whose *Emile* proposed a new order of education, sent his own five children to a home for foundlings.[7]

Politicians have fared no better. A journalist for *U.S. News & World Report* editorialized: "The old affluent, liberal elites spoke left but lived right. And the people of Middle America paid."[8]

The examples run on of those who shape our way of thinking but don't live by their own philosophies. The irony is that many reporters who target preachers and tar-and-feather them in the newspapers for having income that exceeds what they think is correct, turn around and laud lewd and perverse performers who make millions. Certainly, some ministers are guilty of excess or lust, but the media's abuse of reporting practices shows how many simply want to drag Christianity down to their level rather than face the conviction of the Holy Spirit in their own lives. Those of us who want to be real men must seek to live on a higher level and recognize these substitution tendencies, bracing ourselves with truth and reality. Jesus *is* truth! Therefore, Jesus *is* reality!

I was leaving a Christian men's event one day after several hundred men had experienced a powerful movement of God. One man said to me, "Well, it's back to the real world now."

"What do you mean?" I asked. "This *was* the real world! Everything else hinges on what just happened here!"

We cannot be deceived into believing that the circumstances of life are the sum total of our existence on earth. To do so is to cut ourselves off from the reality of the supernatural and the truth that we were created as spiritual beings. Real men recognize truth and cling to it. Unlike the Pharisees of Jesus' day, who substituted religion for relationship, real men recognize Truth, submit to Truth, and are discipled by Him who is called Truth.

There are secular Pharisees today who justify every inconsistency that finds its way into society. They are like those Jesus addressed centuries ago:

> "For John the Baptist came neither eating bread nor drinking wine, and you say, 'He has a demon.' The Son of Man has come eating and drinking, and you say, 'Look, a glutton and a winebibber, a friend of tax collectors and sinners!'" (Luke 7:33–34)

A friend of mine living in Yelm, Washington, said there were people paying as much as $1,500 for "channelling," trying to get a spiritual "high" for their money, using spirits not of God for supernatural direction. Yet there were complaints locally about offerings taken in the churches and how they were used for missionary enterprises.

In some places it is illegal to fly an American flag, but not illegal to burn one. In Rhode Island, a witches' coven was recently recognized as a religion and given tax exempt status, the same status as the godly of the land.[9]

Men make substitutions in the most intimate parts of their lives— their relationships—then wonder why difficulties beset them. Consider two of these:

- Money for affection: Many men would rather give their wives the checkbook than a warm embrace or loving kiss. It's simply easier to give money than oneself.
- Things for time: Many men would rather buy their children things than spend time with them, even though the giving of self is the evidence of love (John 15:13).

The Church has also made substitutions and, in doing so, lost much of the essence of biblical wisdom, which is vital for a vigorous, productive people. Real men must understand that substitutions are not originals. In the Christian community people substitute:

- Talent for anointing: An evidence of relying on the external rather than the internal. But we must realize that God commits to character, not talent.

• Remorse for repentance: Sorrow for getting caught is not sorrow for having sinned. Human sorrow and godly sorrow are as far apart as hell and heaven (2 Cor. 7:9–11).

• Traditions for commandments: Churchianity and Christianity are incompatible. The Lord Jesus Christ rebuked those who substituted the traditions of men for the commandments of God (Matt. 15:1–11).

• Respectability for righteousness: We are not saved by our culture, but by the blood of Christ. Some people are better by nature than others are by grace, but natural graces are no substitute for saving grace.

• Passion for obedience: Mistaking a mere emotional experience with God as a genuine love of God can cost you your soul. The evidence of love is obedience to the Word. If the Word of God does not have lordship in your life, then Christ is not Lord of your life (John 14:15).

• Status symbols for relationships: Stained-glass windows, spiritual exercises, or other aspects of religious life can never be a substitute for a vital relationship with a living Lord.

Some religious people are not necessarily apathetic or lacking in energy—they are simply indifferent to the Word of God (2 Tim. 4:3–4). Indifference is often a form of rebellion. Ezekiel the prophet suffered such an affront. The people who came to hear him were indicted by the Lord when He told Ezekiel, "You are very entertaining to them, like someone who sings lovely songs with a beautiful voice or plays well on an instrument. They hear what you say but don't pay any attention to it!" (Ezek. 33:32 LB).

The "rich young ruler" of Jesus' day faced the decision to love God or money. Money won (Matt. 19:16–22). Hundreds of years before, Ezekiel pegged the same type of religious people for what they really were: "They talk very sweetly about loving the Lord, but with their hearts they are loving their money" (Ezek. 33:31 LB). They heard the Word but refused to act on it (Ezek. 3:32; James 1:22). Jesus warned: "Not everyone who says to Me, 'Lord, Lord,' shall enter the kingdom of heaven" (Matt. 7:21). Substituting confession for commitment can be damning.

The Church was once the driving force behind politics, social reform, and moral values. It was the central focus and meeting place for whole cities and towns. Today as then, we rightfully preach a godly humility, but unfortunately, often practice an ungodly inferiority. The Church preaches a holiness that requires separation from the world, but practices an isolation which has resulted in our losing our impact on the world. Humility and holiness further the work of the Church in the world. Our substitutions have led to an isolated, inferior Church without the status in the community it formerly commanded.

We substitute works for faith, programs for worship, individual experiences for continual abiding, the instant for the constant, culture for salvation. Many men today substitute remorse for repentance, thinking they are mollifying a jealous God. The merely religious, thinking they do service to God only at church, seek out other things to satisfy their deepest cravings: possessions, power, or prestige, to name a few.

I will never forget the evening Nancy and I dropped in on some friends whose children were now grown and had come home to visit. Part of our purpose was to catch up on the children—what they were doing, where they were, and what was happening to them. As we left that evening, I remember hitting my fist on the steering wheel of the car in frustration and sorrow. Nancy asked what was the matter and I pointed out, "Every one of them talked about the new homes, yachts, sports their children are enjoying—but not one of the children know Jesus as Savior. They are substituting culture for salvation."

Societal substitutes are not new to our day. Back in the times of the kings of Israel, the son of Solomon, King Rehoboam, through compromise weakened the nation, allowing their enemy to raid their Temple, taking all the shields of gold from it. Rehoboam then substituted brass shields for the gold, and in so doing gave us an object lesson (2 Chron. 12:9–10). It represented a substitution of the human for the divine, works for faith, good for best, respectability for righteousness. It was an external evidence of an internal change in relationship to God.

Perhaps the greatest substitution error in the Church is substituting God's unconditional love for His conditional promises. The word *if* is a conditional word in some scriptural promises that we tend to chafe at because we must meet conditions to receive God's blessings. Children fret at having to meet conditions before they can receive the parents' reward also. Nevertheless, to obtain the results of promises that are conditional, we must meet the conditions. Thank God for it, for if God's promises were unconditional and His love conditional, salvation would be impossible. Our salvation is not based on our goodness, but on His gracious, unconditional love.

Sex is no substitute for love, but is the sign of the covenant of marriage. Giving sex for money or things is prostitution. In the same way, loving God only for what He will give us is a form of spiritual prostitution. God does give to us. It is in God's nature to give. He cannot *not* give. But if God didn't give us anything, He would still be worthy and deserving of our love because of Who He is.

I once warned some ministers to be careful they do not teach parishioners, or emphasize to the public, to love God merely because of their desires to obtain gifts from Him. To do so could, in the extreme, make the minister no more than a spiritual pimp and his followers mere prostitutes—loving for hire. It is a substitution of lust (a desire to get) for love (a desire to give).

In our substitutions, we lose the opportunity to satisfy the yearnings of the inner man for true peace in the heart.

God said, "I will give them a heart to know Me" (Jer. 24:7), and He sent Jesus into the world to accomplish that relationship. Intimate relationship is the heart-cry of every life. It is God's goal for our lives. Christ prayed that we might be one with the Father, knowing Him intimately as He did. God has lovingly given of Himself to enable humans to be His friends. To accomplish this, Jesus makes it possible for people to have His righteousness, truth, Spirit, and power that they might enter into a right relationship with Him.

While society is hooked on substitutes, real men go for the real thing—Christlikeness!

Chapter 3
Cracks in the Mirror

M irror, mirror, on the wall, who is the fairest of them all?" cried the wicked witch. But when an answer came that put her second on the list, she wanted to kill number one—Snow White.

Today we still compete for the top spot, but we have changed the rules of the game.

"Image, image, on the wall, make me over all." The shift is subtle, yet critical. Reality doesn't matter. Image, however, does.

Television ads boast "image is everything," but the images projected in mainstream society bypass the real issues of life. Many men are content to become shadows without substance, elevating talent and ignoring character, hanging on to an incomprehensible image. Lost in a blizzard of confused images, they thrust themselves forward with a sort of "pretend" image, trying to convince the world they are something they know they are not, hoping that somehow they will strike upon the right path before they are discovered as imposters. When the pressure catches up to the individual, rehabilitation and counseling target behaviors triggered by the internal struggle, but unless core issues are addressed, the man remains abstracted. The image is vitally important, but it is not everything.

A man can go for the image, or the stuff of life behind the image. The results are a fabricated man, or a real man.

Every man has three identities to deal with: the man he wants others to think he is; the man he thinks he is; and the man he really is. The degree to which these three coincide determines the depth of reality and the amount of peace in one's life.

THE MAN HE WANTS OTHERS TO THINK HE IS

Self-help books are replete with advice on how to change or create images that will convince others that a man is something other than what he is. Businessmen have for years been advised to build a strong image and only recently have been counseled that ethics and character are also important. Advertising agencies earn millions of dollars generating corporate images that attract customers for the client. Publicity firms spend clients' hard-earned cash to create, protect, and project the client image, and often work assiduously to conceal their true identity. Image is big business. Right or wrong, images work!

Throughout the world today, men and nations are trying to remake the depiction of their high government officials and appointees because of the severe difficulties in gaining credibility. These are dream jobs for the public relations firms brought in to bolster tarnished images.

In his book *A Question of Character,* Thomas C. Reeves assesses former U.S. President John F. Kennedy as a man who lacked greatness, but had great public relations: "While he had ample courage and at times showed considerable prudence, he was deficient in integrity, compassion, and temperance."[1]

He reveals John Kennedy as a sexually immoral man. His proclivity for promiscuity is now chronicled in pages of history, as well as scandal and gossip magazines. During his lifetime, the illusion of his moral character and behavior was apparently promoted through public relations double-talk, speech writers' brilliance, and political power bought with family money, but Mr. Kennedy's unfaithfulness was his undoing. Regrettably his wife and children have faced the public shame of his life-style. Fortunately for them, the moral level of the world has fallen so low that his licentiousness is accepted with impunity.

Another recent book, *Silent Coup,* gives a sordid picture of men at the pinnacle of political power as deceitful, unethical, liars, unscrupulous, base, and ominous in their danger to the very country they swore to uphold.[2]

Politicians aside, America as a people suffered a terrible beating to our national image—blighted by Vietnam and Watergate, shattered during the Iranian hostage crisis, diminished as terrorists targeted troops and tourists—American leadership was challenged throughout the world. Then, through a series of events—hosting a heralded Olympics, negotiating successfully for political hostages, staging successful military operations, advancing free enterprise in Communist countries—the American image in the minds of its citizens improved. The restoration of the image of prosperity, patriotism, and productivity became the basis for an overwhelming success in "Operation Desert Storm" and a great sense of unity and national pride.

A good image works in business, government, and private life as well. A gentleman named Robert helped me in the early days of my work with men. He had helped his father's company achieve a greater degree of success than ever before, but he left the firm for a couple of years to improve his image in his dad's eyes. Robert sensed that his father's image of him as a new college graduate didn't change even when his corporate reorganization and ideas succeeded and profited their company. Until Robert earned success elsewhere, his father insisted on treating Robert as though he were the boy he helped through school. Robert's success in another field shattered the image of immaturity his father held and created a new concept of him in his father's mind. The result was that Robert returned and his dad trusted him with the responsibility he was amply capable of handling, something that could never have happened until the change in image occurred.

Perhaps one of the best illustrations of this comes from the pages of Scripture where God intervened in individual and corporate life to elevate a person to leadership. Moses had been the deliverer of Israel from Egypt, led the nation through their desert meanderings, brought supernatural provision to the people, and was a proven commander, conqueror, and champion of the people. Then Moses died and his associate was chosen as his successor.

Joshua was now the country's leader. He had served Moses faithfully and well, discharged his duties willingly, and honored God. However, to take the leadership of a people that even God found truculent, Joshua needed to be seen in a different light than that which was reflected from his relationship to Moses.

"The LORD magnified Joshua in the sight of all Israel; and they feared him, as they had feared Moses, all the days of his life," the Bible records (Josh. 4:14). The magnification process was a change of image in the minds of Israel regarding Joshua. That new perception of him enabled him to exercise authority, which he would not have had if they had continued to think of him only as an associate of Moses. His value in their eyes increased according to their perception of him.

Every successor to a leader must be given new esteem, greater regard and standing, to enable him to begin his task.

Images are as important to the illicit as to the legitimate. A national periodical called my hometown of Newport Beach, California, the "scam capital" of America. Deceitful would-be executives extort fortunes here presenting worthless stocks, nonexistent products, and other ephemeral deals by using eye-grabbing graphics, glossy stationery, authoritative titles, and pretentious addresses to present the image of a successful, legitimate corporation. Disguising the criminal intent helps accomplish the solicitation. The reality contradicts the image.

Noted author Thomas Wolfe reportedly stated the 1980s were the "decade of greed" and the 1990s are the "decade of value." Lost moral values in the 1920s spurred the stock market crash and Great Depression. The same loss of values in the 1980s not only created a financial crisis that will cause suffering for two generations, but could yet cause a worldwide economic disaster. Loss of integrity, ethics, faithfulness, trustworthiness, and a depletion of character are behind it. Ironically, *integrity* is a new buzzword in business.

True integrity is found only in a man's character, not his company brochure or in what he calls himself. This is what separates the *real* men from those with the mere image of manliness.

Larry is a self-styled financier whose father is a minister. He grew up in a godly home with praying parents, but never built his life on a solid foundation of righteous principles, genuine faith, and personal relationship with Jesus Christ. A man of tremendous talent and charismatic charm, he built an image, but never developed the substance of godly character.

Larry impressed a young man named John with his contacts. John invested in Larry's projects and encouraged others to do likewise for promised high returns. The investors didn't see that Larry's personal charm covered up a deceitful character. John and the investors lost everything. When their loss became apparent, Larry was impervious to their plight. His dad, mother, and wife lamely excused away his behavior and glossed over what happened.

The Bible warns not to associate with one who calls himself a "brother" but is an "extortioner" or swindler (1 Cor. 5:11).

When John and the other investors lost every dime, John awakened to the fact he had been conned through a carefully constructed image. John's chagrin was not just his loss, but the huge losses of those he counseled. To John it was a financial rape, and he suffered the consequences. It took him years to recover, while Larry continued his conniving ways with different, unsuspecting people. Larry derived his ability to con people from imitating, not building, the godly character of his parents.

John's misguided counsel to the investors illustrates another important biblical truth: Counselors determine the destiny of kings. Rehoboam, successor to his father King Solomon, illustrates this principle clearly.

When Rehoboam became king, Jeroboam confronted him at the behest of the people to ask for a financial respite by lowering their taxes (1 Kings 12). Rehoboam took up the issue with the aged, wise, experienced men who had served Solomon. Their counsel was to lower taxes so that he might serve a lifetime as king. Rejecting their advice he turned to the young men ascending to power with him, who wanted to be his aides and counselors. They were ambitious, inexperienced, vying for power and prestige, and eager to give an answer pleasing to the king.

Their advice to Rehoboam was to tell the people he was king now, not his father, and that the tax burden would be worse, not better. Rehoboam followed the advice of inexperienced, avaricious young men, and his decision resulted in the loss of favor, stature, authority, and money, and divided his kingdom. He never regained the control he dreamed of. Rehoboam's counselors determined his destiny.

THE MAN HE THINKS HE IS

Take the principle of counsel, add the understanding of the power of images, and you have a combustible combination. It is wise to learn from the mistakes of others. Rehoboam may have believed he was someone other than who he was, based on the input of those around him. Brad is a man I once knew well who succumbed to this. Believing in an image of himself that was not based on reality became his undoing.

Brad started a business with little more than an idea. Over the years it expanded beyond his expectations. Many of those trustworthy friends who started the business with him eventually moved on.

New faces were brought in by new executives, some of questionable character. The quality of people around him changed from those who shared his dream to those who saw an opportunity to benefit themselves.

Brad took financial advice from those who were now close to him. Some gave good counsel in a sincere effort to help Brad, but the opportunists knew they would be unable to enrich themselves until Brad personally had more than they wanted. In their lusts, they told Brad how great he was, what he was worth, what he should have, and encouraged him to acquire more for himself, at the expense of the company.

With a new image of himself created by these seducers, Brad began to engage in fiscal manipulations, taking monies for himself that were not his. As he enriched himself, his counselors also got what they wanted. However, difficulties brought in new personnel and thorough financial audits. Brad was indicted, sentenced, went to jail, lost many of his possessions, and endured public disgrace.

His counselors, though, found new positions and advanced their careers with little regard for Brad. Their counsel was not based on what was good for Brad, but on what was good for them. Brad suffered the consequences, while they reaped the dividends.

We are motivated to become what we imagine ourselves to be. As the man thinks, so he is. Because we strive to live up to the images we create, or those created for us, creating an image is one of the most powerful things anyone can do. Shattering it is the next most powerful. Positive or negative, images have power.

Books, movies, and real lives tell the same story again and again of immature males who are bound to an image created in younger years. Their identity crisis, which must be resolved to reach maturity, is really an image crisis. Athletes, hopelessly clinging to some shadow of "glory days," cheat themselves out of the glory of growing wise and mature as they age.

"The glory of young men is their strength; of old men, their experience," Proverbs states (Prov. 20:29 LB).

According to the apostle Peter, whoever overcomes a man, "by him also he is brought into bondage" (2 Peter 2:19). Men are held in bondage by false images that overcome them. Such images form the basis for idolatry in life.

The way to resist false images of ourselves is by thinking correctly, which comes from "renewing your mind" as the Word of God permeates your thought life and the life of Christ permeates your being.

THE MAN HE REALLY IS

Where can we men find the image of real manhood apart from God, who created all human beings "in His image"? And where do we find the knowledge of God but in the Church? The Church desperately needs knowledge and "real men" to teach that knowledge to floundering men and teen-men. Yet, the mores of society impose themselves on the Church, rather than the Church setting the standard for the world.

During recent strife within one denomination, a church official publicly advised that "the Bible is obsolete and too paternalistic. Culture should set our standards, not Scripture." How arrogantly fatuous to regard God's revealed truth as obsolete! Allowing culture to create the blueprint for human behavior is like trying to build the Empire State Building on the ocean. Cultural values change with the times, unless they are built on an absolute standard. And without moral absolutes, everything becomes relative. Relatives are as unhelpful as an unanchored buoy for someone lost at sea.

End-times Bible scholars have prophesied for years that people will one day bow in worship to the "image of the beast" (Rev. 13). That image was thought of as some statue, icon, or monument. Now we realize people can be deceived into worshiping some symbol, logo, or concept created by modern-day "image makers." The image of the "beast" or "system" will one day be projected so that the minds of men and women will embrace its philosophy, and their hearts will be enslaved to its rule. The truth behind that image will be evil, but the image it will project will be one of peace, hope, and concern for others.

With the confused images in the world, the power behind the images, and the knowledge that one day the entire world will be deceived into believing a lying image, men must come to an understanding of the most critical true images of reality—the Image in which they were created—God's image. That's an image worthy of emulation. It can change our inner man.

TRUE GREATNESS

Men and nations are not great by virtue of their wealth, but by the wealth of their virtues.

The moral character, which denotes real manhood, emanates from the inner core of a man's being. "Out of [the heart] spring the issues of life" (Prov. 4:23). And the man who has revealed that character most completely and consistently is Jesus Christ.

Jesus came to earth as the express image of God. He knew in whose image He was created, and who He represented. As such, He was secure in His identity. Because of His "real" manhood, men who find themselves in Him discover true security in identifying with Him even today. He, in turn, begins to reshape them in His perfect image.

Being a Christlike man, being a "real" man, adhering to the true image of manhood in which we were created is far more than running around professing to be "born again" or calling yourself "Christian." I like what a coach said about the great running back Barry Sanders in his rookie year of football. "Barry's not the type of guy who scores a TD and kneels down in front of everyone in the world. He's not for show; he's for real."[3] Thank God for those with the courage to kneel after the game, and even more for those who are willing to live the life every day. One way we live such a life daily is through our words.

Words are the expression of a man's nature, just as God's Word is the expression of His nature. "In the beginning was the Word, and the Word was with God, and the Word was God" (John 1:1). Christ came as the Word incarnate. He was the very expression of God to all people (Heb. 1:3; Col. 1:15).

We can use words for good or ill. But our words say volumes about our true character. For example, on the negative side, profanity is an attitude of heart that expresses itself in one way through words. Profanity is basically taking the name of the Lord in vain. God's commandment is, "You shall not take the name of the LORD your God in vain" (Exod. 20:7). As morality wanes in public life, profanity proliferates. One can hardly shop for a birthday card or read a journal without being confronted with profane words.

Taking the name of the Lord in vain can be done both in word and action. Esau was a "profane person" because he traded his God-given birthright for a bowl of stew (Gen. 27; Heb. 12:16). He was willing to take in vain his eternal inheritance and trade it for material substance—substituting sacred for secular, spiritual for temporal.

Profaning the name of the Lord can be done in other, perhaps even more damning, ways. For example, let's say hypothetically that a friend in Cleveland calls me and says he has just met my wife. My surprised reply is that Nancy has not been in Cleveland. Then I come to find out the woman he met is an imposter to whom I have never spoken nor given permission to use my name. I fly to Cleveland, find her, and ask why she is using my name.

"I like the way you talk so I just started calling myself Mrs. Cole," she replies. Or maybe she answers, "I asked a friend and she said it was all right if I used your name."

By assuming my name immorally and illegally, without my authority or permission, she is profaning my name—taking my name in vain. Think of how people can do the same thing with God. Many call themselves Christians without ever having a personal relationship with Jesus Christ. They do not understand that no one but Christ Himself has the right to give permission to bear His name. When a person repents of sin, believes on Jesus Christ, is "born of His Spirit," and establishes a personal relationship to Jesus Christ, he or she then has the right to be called a Christian. Taking that name by any other means is to profane His name. No one has the right to tell another he may call himself a Christian—Christ has reserved that for Himself.

We can cover our nature by projecting an image we want others to believe, or we can have our nature changed by identifying ourselves with the person of Jesus Christ. Then we are "reborn" as men who are truly made in the "image of God."

But who is this Jesus, anyway? Let's take a close look.

Part 2

The Real Man

∎ ∎ ∎

Chapter 4

Jesus: The Man

*E*cce Homo!

"Behold the Man!"

Jesus was "found in appearance as a man" (Phil. 2:8). Whatever else Jesus was, He was a Man. God the Father declared Him to be the "Son of Man." Jesus was presented to the world in His hour of trial as *the* Real Man!

Even Pilate, the governor of Roman-occupied Israel, announced to the world that he had seen a real man (John 19:5). He had seen many men in their times of crisis before his tribunal, sentenced and pronounced judgment upon them, seen their character unveiled before his eyes as the pressure melted all pretense. But when Pilate saw Jesus, it was with awe and respect.

Pilate looked for a way to avoid the demands of the crowd, but he was political to the core—an expert in the art of compromise, always able to do whatever was expedient to maintain his position and power. So he bowed to the people, but not before they knew his thoughts and feelings regarding the Man they wanted crucified: "I find no fault in him," he declared. When Pilate washed his hands before the angry multitude crying for the crucifixion of Jesus, he was trying to show the religious leaders and the people that he wanted no part of the blood of that just Man on his hands (Matt. 27:24). Pilate then had "King of the Jews" written in Latin, Greek, and Hebrew (John 19:19–20). These were the languages of government, culture, and religion. Thus he announced to peoples everywhere who Jesus was.

Jesus was born in a manger, grew up in a carpenter's home, and worked in the shop. He lived the life of a peasant, yet with royal demeanor. He had no home of His own during His ministry, yet He rarely lacked lodging or food. He died upon a cross as an enemy of the government and was buried in a borrowed tomb. Yet, throughout His entire walk on this earth, He carried the realization of a purpose greater than living itself.

Jesus lived thirty-three years. Thirty years were preparation for the three of public ministry. When He spoke of the virtue of patience, He had lived it. Never premature, either in His actions or speech, He waited until it was time. Patience is the virtue of preparation.

His "life was the light of men" (John 1:4), His path one of righteousness, His work marked by eternity, and He showed all of this and more in His every utterance, attitude, and influence.

Jesus Christ was the most virile and vital of men. Rather than the soft, spineless, wimpish, docile man so often painted—either in word or picture—by misguided writers and artists, He was a man's man. He could act with great gentleness and genuine compassion toward a widow, the sick, or needy; but when confronted by bigotry and hypocrisy His white-hot anger could blaze with righteous indignation.

When He saw the Father's house of worship defiled by the dishonesty and fraud of the "money-changers," in His indignation He drove them out and sought to restore His Father's house as one of prayer (Matt. 21:12).

His wisdom confounded the religious scholars, rebuked the legalists, and revealed the true nature of God as Father to those who believed on Him. He told the religious leaders that their insincerity and hypocrisy would keep them from heaven while repentant publicans and harlots would be welcomed in. The Pharisees were excoriated as "whitewashed tombs," "serpents," and "vipers," because they prayed long and loud to be heard by all. Yet, in private, they stole from the aged and weak (Matt. 23:13–33).

When confronted by religious zealots, eager to show their sancti-monious piety, He exposed their true nature for the world to see. They dragged a woman before Him, whom they said they found in the "very act of adultery," insisting that according to the law of Moses she should be stoned, and they challenged Him to see what He would say or do. (Probably, if it were me, my first question would have been to ask them how they knew where to find her!)

Boldly looking them eye to eye He said, "He who is without sin among you, let him throw a stone at her first" (John 8:7). One by one, they all backed away, leaving the woman standing only with Jesus. Yes, she was a great sinner, but she stood in the presence of a great Savior. Jesus quietly and graciously said, "Neither do I condemn you; go and sin no more" (John 8:11).

A Man of grace, chivalry, and gentleness to those in need. How-ever, His acute sense of right and wrong left Him unafraid to rebuke those deserving it regardless of their status or stature. Even when He was confronted by cynicism and disbelief in His hometown, He re-mained undaunted. "No prophet is accepted in his own country" was His wise perception in the midst of indignity (Luke 4:24).

He was not afraid of them. When they rejected His announce-ment of anointing that equipped Him for ministry, He merely passed through the midst of them. The splendor of His person was such that no man dared touch Him (Luke 4:30).

His perfectly balanced life revealed a dignity unrivaled by any other historical figure, before Him or after. His strengths, revealed in His relationships, first found their basis in the security of His identity. He knew who He was, what He was about, and what He was to accomplish.

Jesus never lost His composure. He suffered the most humiliating indignities ever heaped on anyone. But from the cross He looked down through His incredible pain and saw His mother standing with His disciple John, and in the most tender way told him to take care of her as if she were his mother (John 19:26–27).

Jesus was never disconcerted by human opposition or some im-proper or offensive action or attitude. He never acted hastily or foolishly. He was poised and balanced at all times. There was a finish and completion about Him that caused men to admire Him and women to respect Him.

His life was deeply rooted in prayer. Jesus's greatest source of preparation was prayer. When others demanded action, He was patient in prayer. He knew the Kingdom He was building would continue long after He left the earth and that what He did must be done according to the Father's will. His submission to the Father's will took place in prayer before it evolved into deeds.

Jesus knew better than anyone what it meant to "move the arm of God in prayer." Intercession was not an activity for Him, but a way of life. To assure Himself of right decisions He spent entire nights in prayer (Luke 6:12–13). In preparation for His greatest trial at Calvary, He prayed until His pores bled, with blood like sweat, from His brow. The intensity of His prayer life is forever understood from that long lonely night in Gethsemane (Luke 22:39–46).

Jesus knew our strengths and frailties, our possibilities and limits. His human management techniques were designed to develop the maximum potential of those who followed Him. His training and management abilities were of such great caliber that His trainees literally altered the course of history.

Whenever He spoke, His counsel was not scattered, vague, or inept. He declared truth. To the rich, selfish, and covetous, He said that it was easier for a camel to go through the eye of a needle than for them to get into heaven (Matt. 19:24). Even Peter felt the sting of truth when Jesus said, "Get behind Me, Satan" (Matt. 16:23). He clearly told Peter he was acting like the devil and needed to change.

Though viewing the world collectively, Jesus took care of people individually. His great eternal philosophical perspective might be espoused one minute, and the next He could spend time with a mother who brought her baby to Him. Simplicity and humility marked His life. He was never too busy to meet the needs of whoever came to Him.

Jesus clearly stated to the religious world that social action toward the needy, impoverished, imprisoned, and homeless was an action taken on His behalf. It was a bold, brave, and gallant declaration in the face of those whose only concern was their self-conceived sense of righteousness (Matt. 5:31–46).

"Inasmuch as you did it [acts of kindness] to one of the least of

these [the hungry, naked, sick, imprisoned, and strangers] My brethren, you did it to Me" (Matt. 25:40). Modern-day humanitarians did
not invent social consciousness. Jesus did, and He made it a bedrock
component of the Church. Throughout the world the greatest acts of
charity, monies invested, lives sacrificed, have come from men who
have accepted the will of God for their lives in carrying out the commands of Christ.

Jesus's love knew no bounds and His forgiveness no limits.

When taking His last supper with His disciples He noticed that
they didn't exhibit the common courtesy of washing the feet of
guests. None had offered to do it for Him. Rather than rebuke them
for their oversight, He took pail and towel and in humility began to
wash their feet (John 13:1–17).

Again, Peter tried to rebuke the Lord for attempting to do such a
servile, menial, and humble task. But Peter needed a lesson in humility (John 13:8).

True nobility is realized in true humility.

Jesus taught that a man is only qualified to lead to the degree he is
willing to serve (Matt. 20:26–28).

Humility is not found in self-demeaning attitudes or speech, but
in the willingness to be anonymous. Anonymity is the essence of
humility.

Time after time Jesus instructed those He healed and helped to go
their way and not tell everybody about what happened (Mark 1:44).
He wanted all glory to be given to the Father, because He knew that
people would want to glorify Him on earth (John 6:15). He came to
give glory to the Father, knowing that the Holy Spirit would glorify
Him when the Spirit came to dwell in His followers. His time was not
come, He constantly told His disciples (John 7:6).

Jesus didn't just teach people; He trained them. To train you must
invest time, give of yourself, impart understanding, develop skills in
your students, and motivate them to make others into followers who
in turn lead others.

What Jesus accomplished in three brief years has spanned the
pages of history, rewritten the story of humanity, and given eternal
meaning to every human life. Because of the redemptive nature of
His work, the nature of His own person, too often the manhood of
Christ is minimized.

Look at all the great men of history. Those whose accomplishments in the arts, literature, science, commerce, music, government, and religion are posted in the historical archives of nations. Which of them has established a moral kingdom that will never end?

That Christ did it, and is still doing it, is testified to by the continuing sacrificial devotion and moral victory of people who follow Him today. And two thousand years from now, this Jesus will still rule and reign in people's hearts, whether on earth or in heaven. No one has ever or will ever do what this one single Man has done.

That Jesus established His kingdom on earth by the moral perfection of His life and proved Himself the "power of God to salvation" (Rom. 1:16) is beyond controversy to those who believe. To those who do not believe, He is the most controversial figure in human history.

The reverence created by His person issues in the regard that exalts Him, giving Him a Name above every name, and one day He will cause every knee to bow before Him and every tongue to confess He is Lord to the glory of the Father (Phil. 2:10–11).

Noble yet humble, dignified yet unassuming, gracious yet indignant at injustice, tender yet tough, holy yet human, confrontational yet compassionate, truthful yet understanding, filled with wisdom, He exemplified all that is best in humanity. He is the epitome of real manhood.

Chapter 5
Jesus: The Pattern of Life

On the sixth day of creation, Genesis records God made the first man and first woman in His own image and likeness (1:26–28). That claim is not made of anything else God made. Man and woman alone were created to reflect the Creator in a unique way. So when the first humans walked the earth, they represented God to the rest of creation. But this incredible, one-of-a-kind creation did not go unchanged. It soon suffered an identity crisis. Genesis records this portion of the story in simple but profound detail.

A serpent—Satan in snake's clothing—enticed Eve to cross the only boundary God had established for her and her husband. She ate from the forbidden tree. Then she did what humans have tragically repeated untold numbers of times—she encouraged Adam to follow her footsteps and make the same mistake. He listened and did. Humanity has never been the same since.

Humankind's perfect representation of a perfect God became terribly imperfect. The clear reflection of deity in humanity was darkened with lies, murders, adulteries, betrayals, sufferings, wars, divorces, abuses of every kind. Relationships became guarded; self-interest and self-protection reigned. Innate, absolute moral codes were replaced by external laws often motivated by greed, injustice, and the expedient. Worship of the true God collapsed into worship of false gods of every shape, size, temperament, sex, and (im)moral persuasion. God's perfect, clear image in man and woman was badly marred. It still came through on occasion through acts of self-sacrifice, kindness, humility, and the like, but for the most part, the image revealed more about fallen humanity than it did about the holy Lord.

Then came Jesus. Like Adam before sin, He too had an unbroken, unmarred image. Conceived of the Holy Spirit, Jesus came into the world as a perfect representative and revealer of the Creator. In fact, He *was* the Creator. He made all things, including Adam and Eve (John 1:1–3). He came as the Son of God *and* the Son of Man— perfect deity and perfect humanity joined in the Second Person of the Godhead. Real God and Real Man. The image marred by fallen humans returned in unblemished splendor, exposing the darkness of human sin, revealing the light of divine judgment and grace. When people saw Jesus, they saw who God was and what they were created to be. They saw the model of perfect humanity, the only perfect model of real manhood. They saw the Last Adam, the One who came to restore what the first Adam had shattered.

But He was not what they had expected or wanted. Jesus challenged people's preconceptions and brought confusion to their mistaken interpretations. He turned their values upside down and broke their hardened traditions and taboos. Take the religious order of His day, for example.

The religionists hated Him because He did not conform to their expectations of who and how the Messiah would come and act. His very life was a rebuke to their concept of a God who was uncompassionate and bigoted. Supercilious in attitude, cavalier in conduct, arrogant in demand, they tried to trap Jesus to prove Him a liar. When this proved impossible, they found false witnesses to testify against Him, so they could call for His death in the most savage and repulsive way. By such a death they could press their charge before the multitude that He was an imposter, rebel, and liar. Then they, the interpreters of the Law, "true" descendants of Abraham, would be believed rather than this false prophet whom they charged had merely been "Joseph's son" (Luke 4:22). They deprecated His human origin to deny His divinity.

But many people saw Jesus more clearly than their religious leaders did. Consequently they had many opportunities to experience His power and glory.

As Jesus and His disciples were walking one day, they saw a man who had been born blind. Jesus' disciples asked, "Who sinned, this man or his parents, that he was born blind?" (John 9:2). Jesus, always full of grace, did not rebuke them. Instead, His answer was born of understanding and compassion. Telling them that neither the blind man nor his parents had sinned, He explained to them that the Father had given Him works to do, that He must do them, and they must continue to be done as long as His light could be seen.

Giving His prophetic word, He then spat on the ground, made mud of the moisture and dirt, used it as ointment on the man's blind eyes, and instructed him to go wash in the pool of Siloam. When he obeyed, he was immediately able to see (John 9:7).

The reaction was swift and controversial. Some neighbors reported the miracle and stated he was the young man in the neighborhood that had been born blind. They were sure he was the one who had formerly sat and begged by the wayside. Others mocked and scoffed, saying he seemed like the same man, but they didn't believe it. When the young man who could now see heard the comments of the skeptics and unbelievers, he answered, "I am the man!"

He told them of the Man who made him see and how it happened. The crowd wanted to see the Man. "Where is He?" they asked. The healed youth said he didn't know, but he knew he could see. When the bystanders reported it to the religious leaders, they interrogated him about what happened. After he recounted his testimony, they wanted to know where the Man was who had healed him. He didn't know, he told them.

Continuing to mistrust and misconstrue what happened, they finally confronted the young man's parents, demanding to know if his story was true. The parents compromised themselves and their son with an evasive reply, saying he was their son and he was born blind, but denied any knowledge of how he recovered his sight or who had healed him.

Because the miracle had occurred on the Sabbath, no one would admit the healing for fear of reprisal for breaking the Law by working on the Sabbath. In exasperation, the religious leaders called for the young man a final time and commanded him to glorify God, but not Jesus, because they said Jesus was an evil person. The young man said, "Whether he is a sinner or not, I don't know. One thing I do know. I was blind but now I see!" (John 9:25 NIV).

Becoming more strident and fierce in their opposition to the miracle and the undeterred young man, they expressed their faith in Moses, declaring they were his disciples and they did not know about "this Jesus."

"He can heal blind men, but you don't know anything about

Him?" the healed man challenged (my paraphrase). "Strange that nothing like this has ever occurred before, and if this Man were not from God, He couldn't do it" (John 9:30–32).

The religious leaders then insulted him and threw him out of the synagogue (John 9:34).

When Jesus heard what had happened, He found the young man and asked him if he believed in the Messiah. When he asked, "Who is He?" Jesus said, "I am He." With those words ringing in his ears, the young man's eyes beholding the glory of God that he could now see, his heart pounding with joy, he immediately began to worship Jesus (John 9:37–38).

This man did not question that Jesus was the Messiah after the miracle. There was no wondering, second guessing, wanting further proof—just an instant acceptance of the nature of Jesus the Christ.

Jesus's wisdom, power, humility, and identity were evident as He revealed Himself to this desperately needy young man. Though others denied His Lordship, this young man eagerly accepted the disclosure as a discovery of eternal magnitude. To him there was no question concerning Christ, nor his willingness to be a disciple.

Another incident occurred at Calvary where an uncommon man, a soldier, met One who changed his life.

Soldiers are paid to deal with death. Their life is a preparation to live and die. They are taught to kill or be killed. Killing is their vocation. Paid to engage in wars that may even be immoral, their life often begins to reflect those mores. Roman soldiers in occupied countries dealt with citizen resentment, political intrigue, an economic black market, and usually became indifferent in their treatment of those they policed.

Captains of these forces, commissioned to carry out the commands of dictatorial authorities, gave great latitude to soldiers under their command. War is always ugly, and occupation by foreign powers is forever mean-spirited. Such were the Romans occupying Israel at the time of Christ. When the trial of Christ took place, the soldiers mocked, beat, and whipped Him and gambled away His possessions.

The centurion, or captain of the guard, watched with a sardonic attitude. Through it all there was something different about the way Jesus underwent their taunting, torture, and punishment. The centurion saw a surprising manner in Jesus. The witnesses lied about Him, the High Priest reviled Him, and people preferred an obvious criminal to a Man in whom Pilate could find no fault.

When the climactic moment of crucifixion occurred, the veil in the Temple was rent, darkness spread over the land, and people shouted with joy, for in the midst of the gloom they were being healed, and the dead came out of the graves. It was such an incredible event that even the heartless centurion who was executing Jesus could no longer deny that this Man was God.

Experiencing that event, seeing the manner in which Jesus bore ignominious shame while maintaining His love and grace, how He cried out for forgiveness for those who were screaming for His death while He hung on the cross in agony of body and anguish of soul, the Roman centurion finally cried out, "Truly this Man was the Son of God" (Mark 15:39).

The centurion knew men. He commanded them. He understood authority at the highest level and how to use it. In his profession captains go down with the ship, commanders lead their troops into battle to show the way, but to undergo the ordeal of crucifixion as Jesus did made him realize Jesus was more than just a man. He could only be who He said, based on the evidence before the centurion's very eyes. A hardened realist became an ardent disciple. History confirms that the centurion became an active believer, leading his family in the way of the Lord.

Jesus is definitely our model of the Real Man.

His nature, virtue, character, vitality are the epitome of manliness. What He taught and lived became the pattern for masculinity.

To know what a man is, how to live as a man, how to act and react in conduct and attitude, glorify God and heal society, lead a family and nation, build character and develop relationships, love good and hate evil, we must look to Jesus Christ. He is every man's Man.

As a matter of fact, a national magazine recently conducted a survey of men and women in the United States, asking them who best represented their ideal man. Jesus received more votes than any other, from both men *and* women. When asked what qualities set Him apart, the most common responses were a caring attitude, intelligence, admirable morality, and sensitivity to others. Even today's nonreligious society admires these qualities.[1]

But Jesus' perfection poses a problem for the rest of us. We are flawed. Our ability to reflect the image into which we were born has been broken by sin, and we can't repair it on our own. We lack the power or ability to obtain the original endowments in the first man—Adam (Rom. 5:14). So we need more than a role model. We need an infusion of the very spirit, mind, and heart of the embodiment of manhood found in the Last Adam—Jesus Christ. How can we get that? Once again, Jesus paved the way for us.

Because of His prayer to the Father for us to receive His very own Spirit, what the Spirit produced in Jesus can also be reproduced in us. He said that He did only those things He saw the Father do (John 5:19), and by virtue of that we are to do those things we see in Christ, thus accomplishing the Father's will in our lives.

Jesus was given the Spirit without measure (John 3:34); we are given the Spirit by measure. Jesus was sinless; we are sinful. Our right standing with God is really His, imputed to us.

To the extent that we yield our life to Him, His nature and works are reproduced in our lives. We "see in a mirror, dimly" (1 Cor. 13:12), contend with heart conditions and mindsets that continually want to return to the dust from which we were created, but with Christ's resurrection power, we are lifted above them with power over them.

When Moses held his rod in his hand it was to glorify God and accomplish His work on earth. But when he threw it down, it took the form of a serpent. So our human spirit, when held in hand by the power of the Holy Spirit and authority of the Word of God, is something that can bring glory to God. However, when we are not controlled by the Spirit, our mind, heart, and will are "out of hand," uncontrolled, and we revert to an old nature whose desires are contrary to those of God.

The attributes of Christ are the characteristics of true manhood. They are evidences of Sonship to the Father. In their manifestation they reveal the divine flow of the Spirit of Christ, which occurred first in Him, and now in those born of His Spirit.

A divine principle of reproduction revealed in creation is that everything reproduces after its kind. Look at the natural kingdoms of this earth. Oranges reproduce oranges; horses reproduce horses; people reproduce people. That which is "born of the flesh is flesh, and that which is born of the Spirit is spirit" (John 3:6).

Humanity is born of the flesh and does not have divine nature through natural reproduction. That's why Jesus told Nicodemus that he must be born again (John 3:3). He was teaching that to have the impartation of the nature of God, because God is Spirit, we must be born of His Spirit even as we were born of flesh. When the Spirit of Christ comes into a human life, it is a "birthing," being made alive in the Spirit.

In natural birth, without the Spirit of God, there is no life of God, and thus no eternal life in man. Christ came as a light into the world because natural humans depend upon external sources of light. Light that shines on a clear path to walk at night is not something that is naturally produced from man's being. He must have a flashlight or some other capability or source to show the path clearly that he may walk without stumbling.

So man is in need of the light of the soul. Christ is that light. When Christ's Spirit comes into the person, the meaning of life becomes clear where before it was dark and murky. The light of Christ shines surely, showing right from wrong, revealing not only one's true heart condition, but also the nature of God. The brightness of the Word of God becomes an internal beacon to show men the right path of life.

The Old Testament prophets spoke of the coming Christ, and now the New Testament looks back on Him who came. Much greater are those now born into the kingdom of God, entering into a new covenant, than those who lived under the old. Jesus, comparing Old Testament prophets to John said, "Among those born of women there has not risen one greater than John the Baptist; but he who is least in the kingdom of heaven is greater than he" (Matt. 11:11).

Who could take upon Himself such a task, accomplish the divine purpose, reveal God as Father, except the One who is both the Son of Man and Son of God? In His humanity He took part in our flesh; by His Spirit we take part in His divinity, becoming the righteousness of God in Christ Jesus (2 Peter 1:4).

The world seems complex, but it's actually very simple. It is comprised of those who believe and those who don't.

Secular and sacred.

Unregenerate and regenerate.

Those born of the flesh only, and those born of the flesh and Spirit.

Jesus Christ, Son of the living God, makes the difference.

Scripture is definite: "He who believes in the Son has everlasting life; and he who does not believe the Son shall not see life, but the wrath of God abides on him" (John 3:36).

Even the human heart is hopelessly deceived (Jer. 17:9). Only God's Word can reveal the true nature and heart of a person. The Bible acts as a mirror reflecting the real person, showing the need for change. Whereas most of societal efforts for change are superficial, God deals directly with the truth in the light of Christ. Jesus came as the "light of the world" (John 8:12; 9:5). As light makes manifest what was hidden in darkness, so in the light of God's Word the true condition of the human heart is made manifest (John 3:20–21). God glories in the man who comes to Him humbly, honestly seeking change to be conformed to the image of manhood as found in Jesus Christ, made into a "real man."

Having divested Himself of the glory He had in heaven, humbling Himself to be made a little lower than the angels, made in the likeness of humanity and of no reputation, He became like us as men, to show us how to live (Phil. 2:5–8; Heb. 2:7–8). Having depended entirely on the Holy Spirit to live life, He made it possible for us to receive that same Holy Spirit into our lives so we can live as He did on this earth. He commanded His disciples to do the same works He did through faith (John 14:12). By doing so men will glorify God as He did. Only then will the real meet the ideal, finding fulfillment and satisfaction in the maturing process of manhood, and in that state a man will become the same to others as he is to himself and as he is before God.

Chapter 6

Jesus: The Power of Life

Communication is the basis of life.

Exchange is the process of life.

Balance is the key to life.

Agreement is the power of life.

These are the four principles that every man needs to understand. They are essential to life.

Communication of the sun's power to earth causes plant photosynthesis that produces organic food for human consumption; pollen is carried by wind, insects, water, and other agents to impregnate plants and produce seeds; animals and people alike establish some form of communication as a prelude to reproduction.

Both business and marriage are based on proper communication. Education is based on communication and without it knowledge would cease. Today we live in an information age, a shrinking world, and a global community, due to new methods of communication.

Without the Bible's telling us of Jesus, we would be eternally bereft of God's grace. His Spirit communicates to us that we are children of God.

Agreement is the power of life because, without it, both authority and ability would be lost. Marriage is based on two parties agreeing to live together until death parts them. Builders are restricted in construction unless they have an agreement between parties and civic authorities.

Until humans agree with God's assessment of them and His provision for their eternal benefit, they are without His authority and ability. As they live in agreement with His Word by faith, His power is released in their lives.

"A house divided cannot stand" is the principle Jesus gave in Scripture (Matt. 12:25). "Unite my heart to fear Your name," cried the psalmist (Ps. 86:11). Disagreement results in powerlessness; agreement produces power.

Companies that have employees in agreement with their policies and united in a common effort produce great profits. When disunity, confusion, and misunderstanding develop, they lose their ability to produce.

Patterns and principles such as these have been part of my life since they came alive to me during a forty-day fast. They are biblical truths that find their origin in Jesus Christ.

He is God's communication to us; Calvary is the place where Christ exchanged His righteousness for our sinfulness that we might give up our sinfulness for His righteousness. Jesus gives the balance of repentance and faith which unlock heaven and made an agreement or new covenant with God by which we are assured of eternal life.

The process of exchange is the process of life. We inhale oxygen and exhale carbon dioxide from our lungs, while the blood system carries nutrients and oxygen to the cells of the body, and the veins carry away waste products of metabolism. The exchange made in these processes gives life to our bodies.

In another very real way, exchange takes place through crises. Birth, in which you exchange the womb for the world, is a crisis, but it is normal to life. Through the major crises of life, maturity increases until death, which is the final crisis. A close friend of mine says, "Crisis doesn't make the man; it only exposes him for what he is."

Each step of maturity or growth generally occurs through some crisis. The only constant in life is change, and change customarily produces crisis.

Each step of growth in a business is accompanied by a crisis: new equipment needed, new personnel hired, facilities expanded or bought, but each in turn produces a crisis, either small or large, expected or unexpected. The exchange of the old for the new is usually acceptable (though not always welcomed at first) for the benefit it brings.

As a relationship ripens, deepens, becomes more intimate, the accompanying crises are often the means of making it possible. Going from a transient state to a more permanent one is, as a rule, occasioned by crisis.

Marriages develop and mature as each partner comes to a greater understanding of the needs and desires of the other. More often than not, it doesn't begin until a crisis occurs and forces discussion and they discover each other's attitudes so that changes between them can occur. That's why communication is the basis of life. When it stops, all hope of reconciliation is curtailed.

A flower on a plant derives its existence from the sap flowing through the roots. When it is severed from its stem, an abnormality sets in and without reconciliation the ultimate end of the flower is death. It's a part of life. Cessation of communication from the roots to the flower causes death. Likewise, when communication stops between married partners, the marriage dies. The result is often divorce.

There are many forms of death: physical, mental, social, economic, emotional, or even spiritual. With the Lord Jesus Christ, death was a process of exchange both for our benefit and that of Almighty God, to take us from the transient state of life on earth to a permanent place with Him in heaven.

Through His death and resurrection, Jesus broke the power of the devil, who through sin had the power of death, and brought freedom to all people, who had been living as slaves to the constant dread of death.

Consider with me some propositions concerning death.

First: To the Christian, death is only a transition from one state of being to another that is higher. It's the crisis by which we go from a transient to a more permanent state of being. Crisis is normal to life because it is the catalyst for change. Death is the ultimate crisis in life, and any death of any kind is a crisis.

Second: Death is only an enemy when death occurs outside Christ. In Christ death and life are both servants (1 Cor. 3:2 LB). Death is the necessary intermediary in bringing a greater dimension to life. Death in Christ is only a process of exchange—the terrestrial for the celestial; mortal for immortal; natural for spiritual; corruptible for incorruptible (1 Cor. 15:53–54).

Life is born out of death in the same manner in which success is born out of failure. Jesus taught that He could not give life except through His death at Calvary. The devil tried to deceive Him into a compromise by offering Him all the kingdoms of this world if He would only bow down and worship him. (Satan's goal has always been to replace God.) Jesus refused.

Third: Any death in Christ must be followed by a resurrection or it is not in Christ. The crucifixion is incomplete without the resurrection. He "was delivered up because of our offenses, and was raised because of our justification" (Rom. 4:25). God not only called believers to live a crucified life, but a resurrected life through Jesus Christ. The resurrection took away death's victory.

Fourth: The resurrection is the ultimate miracle. If you believe in the resurrection you can believe for any miracle. Every miracle flows from the same power that manifested the glory of God by raising Christ from the dead.

Fifth: Jesus established a principle when He said, "He who finds his life will lose it, and he who loses his life for My sake will find it" (Matt. 10:39). He was simply saying that if we are willing to die to self and this present evil world ("filled with lust and rottenness" is how Peter put it [2 Peter 1:4 AB]), and throw our total dependence upon Him, we shall find life. Everlasting life!

Sixth: For the Christian there are many forms of dying to self. Repentance is a form of self-death. So are intercession and fasting. Virtually any form of self-sacrifice, no matter how small, involves death to self.

Seventh: Financial death can occur in many ways, but in many countries it is mitigated by bankruptcy laws. Such laws are usually a shadow of the substance found in the Old Testament "Year of Jubilee" the Lord established for the economic future of the nation of Israel. "Jubilee" was when debts were forgiven, lands restored, and people had an opportunity to start anew (Lev. 25:8–55). Such forgiveness was symbolic of death and resurrection.

Eighth: There is death, and there is a "spirit of death." The spirit of death is akin to symptoms of illness. Symptoms are not always diseases in themselves, but often are merely invitations to have the disease. When resisted, denied, and rebuked they have no effect. The "spirit of death" is often just an oppression to submit to death, but when reproved in the name of Jesus, it cannot claim its prey.

Having stated these propositions, let's look at the life of a great "man of God," Elijah, and see what happened to him. He contended with the wicked and evil Jezebel and her prophet-priests who were defiling and deceiving the people of her country. She dominated her husband, seduced her nation, and was infuriated that she could not counter the influence of Elijah.

Engaged in a contest with her priests, Elijah emerged triumphant, proving that Jehovah was God, but ran miles from the scene to escape Jezebel's threat to kill him. Now, much later, wearied with his labors, exhausted from the journey, he sat down under a juniper tree and commiserated with himself.

In his depression he asked to die, and said, "It is enough; now, O LORD, take away my life; for I am no better than my fathers" (1 Kings 19:4 KJV). Therein lies the fivefold temptation that men suffer and in which the spirit of death desires to take hold of men's lives:

(1) Depression
(2) Despair
(3) Inferiority
(4) Resignation
(5) Failure

God didn't let Elijah die, but helped him recover, caused the spirit of death to leave him, then raised him up to pass his mantle to Elisha and exchange his juniper tree for a chariot of fire.

During my lifetime I have suffered those temptations, watched great men go through the agonizing process, and gloried each time renewed vigor and vitality flowed into the life.[1]

Failing is not the worst thing in the world; quitting is.

The apostle Paul knew the dilemma and frustration of wanting to do right but being unable to do it. "For the good that I will to do, I do not do; but the evil I will not to do, that I practice" (Rom. 7:19). He felt trapped and needed out of it. He was powerless. He needed help.

Then after knowing Christ he said, "For the law of the Spirit of life in Christ Jesus has made me free from the law of sin and death" (Rom. 8:2).

Delivered from his bondage to sin, the past still paraded before him. In his zeal to persecute Christians, he had had them thrown into prison, some killed, and some even stoned. Now that he was a believer, he sat in the place of worship with widows made that way by his religious hatred, and with men whose sons were lost through his persecution of them. The guilt of his past was a burden too heavy to bear. He compared himself to those judged guilty of premeditated murder.

The punishment at the time for someone convicted of deliberately plotting murder, tried, and found guilty is unusual to us but fits the crime. The body of the victim was chained to the guilty, and wherever the convicted murderer went, he dragged the dead body with him. Ostracized by the community, he found it difficult to survive.

Eventually the weight of the dead body, guilt of the deed, exclusion from society, isolation from normalcy, separation from family and friends killed the condemned person. That's how Paul described his condition, as if chained to his past sin, guilt, and shame. They were a weight too heavy to bear, and if not released from them they would eventually kill him.

Then he found his freedom from the same source that brought him the good news of his salvation—the Lord Jesus Christ. Writing for all the world to know, he said, "Thanks be unto God through Jesus Christ my Lord." *He was free!*

Freed from his chains to the past, he later wrote in a letter to a church, "Forgetting those things which are behind and reaching forward to those things which are ahead, I press toward the goal for the prize of the upward call of God in Christ Jesus" (Phil. 3:13–14).

Death to sin set him free to live. By dying to the past he was free to live in the present with a great hope in the future. In Christ, death is a servant to bring the greater life through resurrection power.

Dying is never easy. In any form.

My mornings usually start at 6:30 A.M. on the beach near my house. There with Jack Mackey, my prayer partner, I spend the first hour or so in prayer. Months of faithfully applying ourselves to seeking God brought a remarkable change in Jack's life. We have worked together for almost twenty years, but today he is a different man from the one I used to know. One day on the beach when I was away, Jack was convinced by Scripture that he had practiced rationalizing truth for a lifetime. Because he always wanted to look good in his own eyes, he avoided confrontation, or issues that made him look bad, and "skirted the truth."

The Holy Spirit convicted him of being a liar. He thought he would die. Raised in the church and now in the ministry, lying was contrary to everything he had ever thought of himself or even considered. A gigantic battle ensued in his mind and heart. He knew he needed to confess that sin, but to admit he was a liar was more than he could bear.

"If God had called me a thief, murderer, or anything else, it would not have affected me as deeply," Jack recalls. "But when He convicted me of being a liar—it was like death itself." He remembers vividly four days of wrestling in his heart and mind, until he finally stood on the jetty at the beach and shouted, "I am a liar!"

"When I admitted it, something went out of me," he says. "It was like I passed from 'death unto life.' I have never experienced anything like it in my life. In the months since, it seems that for the first time in my life the Lord is speaking to me personally from His Word. I know what it is to 'eat the Word.' It is sustenance to my soul—I am alive!"

His dying was to admit his sin, but the dying brought resurrection. He lives on a higher level today, walking in the Spirit, a level he would never have experienced if he had not repented.

Jack is not an isolated case in human study. There is not a man I know who is successful in ministry today that at some point in his life did not go through an experience where he had to die to himself and all that he had, but through it found a greater scope and degree of life and ministry than ever before.

Let me tell you something right now, and consider this carefully.

If you have suffered the loss of a job, been through the agonies of divorce, suffered bankruptcy, lost a friend or loved one—when you commit and submit that to Christ, know this—there will come a resurrection for you!

Just as the sting of death is removed by the resurrection, so the sting of failure is removed by success.

The greatest evidence of the faith of Jesus was when He trusted the Father to raise Him from the dead. When it came time to die, Christ trusted Himself into the Father's hands totally and completely, believing that God would raise Him from the dead. He had no fear of death because of His faith in the Father (Luke 22:41–44).

Faith is similar to wind—you can see neither of them—only the results of their presence. That's why James wrote, "I will show you my faith by my works" (James 2:18). Faith is only seen by its works.

Have faith in God, not in symptoms, signs, symbols, or circumstance. The Word of God is your foundation of faith. Experience only serves as a witness to faith's results.

Don't let the past weigh you down!

Don't let a disaster become your grave!

Die to those things that you might live!

If you have never repented, died to self by admitting wrong, do it so God can raise you from death in trespasses and sins.

The resurrection life is glorious in its unlimited freedom and expression.

Before I leave this subject let me add one thing concerning men in ministry. Every minister wants to succeed, to be successful. Most generally train in schools that teach doctrine, language, and technical aspects of ministry. Teaching to succeed, how to achieve, how to live is fine, but the real secret of successful ministry is not in the living; it's in the dying to self. Professors teach everything except the one necessary ingredient that makes living glorious and ministry successful.

It's true in every aspect of living.

Marriage is successful because each partner dies a little to him- or herself to make the marriage successful. Most successful businessmen have died through failure before succeeding.

Death brings the resurrection.

The resurrection is worth the dying.

Christ died that we might have life "and . . . have it more abundantly" (John 10:10). Everyone wants the abundant life, but not the death that makes it possible. You can't have one without the other. Death and resurrection go together. The cross and the empty tomb are incomplete without one another.

Now is the time—submit and commit your life to the Lord—repent of sin and receive His resurrection life.

You will have an entire eternity to enjoy it.

Part 3
Real Sight

■ ■ ■

Chapter 7
Life-Changing Values

When God created men and women in His image and moral likeness, He endowed us with five powerful characteristics that enable us to live a Christlike life, thereby bringing some of heaven to earth. The five characteristics are:

(1) Capacity to know truth
(2) Ability to recognize moral excellence
(3) Power to exercise our will
(4) Creative power in our words
(5) Right and ability to reproduce

For the Christlike man, these attributes aid in the stewardship of earth and family, to fulfill the will of God, accomplish His purposes, and glorify Him. As these God-given abilities bring glory to God, they also bring remarkable blessings to individual human life, society, and whole cultures. However, men today, though more enlightened and cultured than any people in history, as a whole, neither

recognize nor use these God-given endowments to enrich life and
bring glory to God on earth, which is evident by the state of nations
today.

The U.S., for one, is losing its God-given uniqueness. Begun by
diverse groups of people seeking religious and economic freedom,
the U.S. has now lost sight of her God-blessed beginnings. John Anderson, in his book *Cry of the Innocents,* writes that America shows
remarkable similarities to the pattern that brought Israel down during
the time of Hosea:

(1) Became victim of the culture around them
(2) Seduced by pagan worship, saw little harm or difference in
religious practice
(3) Thought Canaanites had the better life
(4) Lost sense of God's presence and purpose
(5) Embraced "fertility cults"; their sexual promiscuity led to a
moral breakdown of society
(6) Moral degeneration led to murder[1]

Lower morality leads to higher mortality. Instead of laying down
life to ensure greater life, men may take life because life is deemed
valueless. In Nazi Germany where a similar breakdown occurred,
the result was the Holocaust. In America today the holocaust is
called abortion. In other nations where genocide occurs in civil
wars, the value of human life is just as negligible.

John Anderson explains in his new book, *Cry of Compassion:*

The cry for a father is the cry to be wanted. If the 1940s produced
the postwar generation, the '50s the silent generation, the '60s the
dropout generation, the '70s the rebelling generation, the '80s the
self-centered generation, then in the '90s we are reaping their
fruit: We are producing the "unwanted generation." From abortion
to child abuse, from careers to life-style, the message we give our
children is "We don't want you!" That is, we don't want you unless
it is convenient for us! We will allow you to be born at our convenience; and, if you are conceived when it is not convenient, we
will destroy you. And, when we have allowed you to be born, we
will spend time with you when it is convenient. Our children are
learning this message.[2]

You wonder why we are having problems with youth all over the world? They're getting the message: "You have no more value than any other commodity in life."

Not only the value of people, but the value systems themselves, which uphold and give worth and dignity to man, are being destroyed.

God's Word holds the moral principles upon which a strong and prosperous society rests. When Israel adhered to God's precepts they prospered above all nations, but when they set out to be "like other nations," by rejecting Jehovah and demanding an earthly king, they withered internally and the whole nation collapsed. Overrun by other nations, demeaned by wicked kings, Israel lost the glory of their God.

Today moral principles are still inherent in God's Word as the only true value system that sustains life and makes societies worthwhile. Rejection of absolutes makes all rules and regulations relative and slanted to the self-interests of the powerful.

As society degenerates, drifting further from God, it allows humanism, materialism, and secularism to establish its value system as a substitute for that which is God given. The change in the value systems of a people reflects on the entire society. The U.S. economy reflects the values that are far from the values of Jesus Christ. A 1986 survey revealed that America spends:

- $2.5 billion on chewing gum,
- $12 billion on candy,
- $19 billion on lotteries,
- $1.7 billion in total giving to 600 Protestant denominations, which is less than what is spent on Nintendo games.[3]

In their analysis of the vast disparity between what people spend on frivolous items and what they give to spread the gospel, researchers concluded that personal life-style is more important than church life. Church members, who have the gospel by which men are saved from hell, the most important message ever given to the world, affirm or deny its worth by their support of winning souls for Christ. This economic research suggests American Christians no longer value the gospel above all else.

The fall of communism, anarchy in the Soviet republics, and independence of Eastern bloc countries shows the fallacy of atheism.

Sadly, and incongruently, while the Soviet Union receives the Bible with eagerness, the very nation that made it possible—America—is rejecting God's Word and has outlawed the Bible and prayer in public schools.

My grandson has a poster on his wall that reads, "In case of nuclear attack, the ban on prayer in public schools will be temporarily lifted."

Since the injunction against prayer in the public schools, laws in the U.S. have progressively omitted Christianity and moral values from our schools. During this time SAT scores have dropped an average of 70 points, premarital sex has increased, the dropout rate has risen drastically, and American school children have scored steadily lower in international comparisons.[4] The American school system has degenerated into armed camps. What was once a school playground has now become a battleground. Barbed-wire fences surround the schools and armed guards patrol the hallways. Where once love notes exchanged hands at students' book lockers, today drugs are distributed.

Removal of God from human life erodes societal mores and distorts personal value systems by which men live. Christians must develop personal value systems based on the Word of God, apart from society's dictates.

Men must value the will of God above all else. Even before God sent Jesus in the form of a man, Moses esteemed "the reproach of Christ greater riches than the treasures in Egypt" (Heb. 11:26). He left his place in Pharaoh's house in Egypt, following God to an uncertain future in the wilderness. Conversely, hundreds of years later, Demas, one of the first converts to Christianity, renounced his faith in Christ because he "loved this present world" (2 Tim. 4:10). A value held, then discarded denotes a tragedy out of proportion to its telling. But he was not alone.

Esau sold his birthright for a bowl of stew when he came home famished from hunting (Gen. 25:29–34). Physical sustenance meant more to him than his birthright. Later, after maturing, he wanted the birthright back but could not find a place of repentance though he wanted it desperately.

Daniel, on the other hand, held his values even at the expense of his life. Knowing the king had decreed that anyone praying to their God would be sent to the lions' den, Daniel boldly and publicly continued to pray three times a day as he always had. His faith in God held more value than royal threats. When he was thrown into the lions' den, God shut the mouths of the lions. Daniel was delivered, his accusers were slain, and the king glorified God (Dan. 6). Daniel held his convictions and would not recant his faith, though the king and people preferred he would.

Pastor Al Bernard of Brooklyn, New York, teaches the three differences between preference and conviction:

(1) People who live by preference can be negotiated out of their preferences. Convictions are nonnegotiable.
(2) People who live by preference weaken under pressure. Convictions grow stronger.
(3) People who live by preference always dislike those who hold convictions.

When the religious leaders of Jesus's day confronted Him and demanded He stop preaching in their synagogues, healing the sick, forgiving sinners, working miracles, and feeding the poor, He refused. Jesus wasn't ministering because He preferred it, but out of conviction that brought Him to earth from heaven. Jesus knew who He was, why He was here, what God's message was, and where He was going.

Jesus lived by His convictions, not men's preferences.

Consider these propositions concerning life's value systems.

SOME THINGS *ARE* MORE IMPORTANT THAN LIFE ITSELF

Daniel, the prophet-statesman, in his book in the Bible tells of his three friends, the three Hebrew children. Arrogant men, who wanted to replace them in the court, accused and threatened them. They refused to negotiate when confronted with the demand to worship the king or burn in a fiery furnace. Instead, they grew stronger and incurred the wrath of those who lived by preference. Their standing could be seen better when all others were bowing. The king's threats to hurl them into a furnace seven times hotter than usual held no dismay for them. The fiery furnace held no more dread for them than did the lion's den for Daniel. Their convictions gave God the opportunity to "show Himself strong on [their] behalf" (2 Chron. 16:9). When they were finally thrown into the furnace, there was a fourth man with them as they walked about freely, and when the king called for them, they came out unsinged, without even the smell of smoke on their clothes (Dan. 3).

People who live by conviction are considered peculiar by those who live by preference.

Prophets always precede the deliverer. John the Baptist was the forerunner to Jesus. To John the honor of God was more important than his life. When he angered King Herod's wife by pointing out her sin, she told her daughter to ask for John's head. At a banquet, King Herod displayed on a silver platter the head (and values) of John the Baptist (Matt. 14:3–11).

Men have dueled and died defending their honor. Women have died under a rapist's attack, fighting for their virtue, which they esteemed more important than their life. Conversely, perverted values cause addicts to abandon their honor for a few moments of pleasure.

On a far grander scale, Jesus Christ considered our presence in heaven more important than His own life, dying for us while we were enemies of His, to make it possible for us to become the people God created us to be. His basic motivation was love for the Father, His mission was to seek and save the lost, and His ministry is as our Prophet, Priest, and King.

Men who live the Christian life do not count their lives dear to them. Contending for the faith is not a slogan, nor a motto, but a way of life for them. Loss of job, money, career, reputation is a form of death to them, but they risk it gladly for the gospel's sake.

Some cautioned Pat Robertson against taking strong public stands on his Christian beliefs, warning him he might lose the entire Christian Broadcasting Network. He replied, "I started with $70 and I've got at least $100 in my pocket now, so I guess I'm ahead." With that he put in perspective his esteem of the half-billion dollar network he founded. Christ meant more to him than all the achievements, reputation, and possessions accumulated during his life. People live and die by their personal value systems.

THE INTANGIBLE IS MORE IMPORTANT THAN THE TANGIBLE

The internal is more important than the external; the unseen more important than the seen; and the spirit more important than the body (2 Cor. 4:18).

Wisdom is more valuable than rubies; love superior to sex; respect more substantial than money; a good name more to be chosen than riches; honor more valuable than position.

It is not unusual for men who miss the value God places on human beings to regard people as commodities. Professional athletes struggle with that throughout their careers, feeling that they are simply something to be owned, bought, sold, or traded. They press for more money because they believe it is their only measure of respect. To the owners they are just another commodity, without any respect for them as a person—only for their talent—and when that diminishes they are discarded.

One reason for some women's negative attitudes toward men today is that many a woman feels that a man finds value only in her body and she lacks value as a person. True of the prostitute who regards her value as only in the functions her body performs, and she sells herself according to the value she places on herself. Her value generally comes to her first by her father, then other men, and finally her pimp. It's why such women reputedly throw away their lives on drugs, because to them their life seems worthless in their eyes.

A wife often comes to think that her only value to her husband is in service to him, and when she begins to think of herself only in servile terms, she loses value in her estimation of herself.

When a husband views his wife as just another commodity, having no more value than his car, computer, or other possessions, he tends to show her little respect. Some husbands pay more attention and give more time to their cars than to their wives. When a man's car begins to age, show signs of wear and tear, no longer serves him as expected, he begins to look at other models and think of a trade-in. Too often he does the same with his wife, which can account for part of the high divorce rate.

Women have accused men of wanting a lady in the living room, cook in the kitchen, and whore in the bedroom. Respect is an intangible that is more important than the tangible. Respect gives dignity to life. The Lord told the husband to love his wife, and the wife to respect her husband, for you cannot submit to what you do not respect.

I heard the humorous story about the couple who became concerned about his illness. He grew steadily worse, and his wife didn't know whether he would live or die. Concerned, she took him to a doctor who spent an entire day on tests and examinations while she waited. When he finally appeared, she asked him what the doctor said about his condition. "He didn't say," was his reply.

"Well, I want to know," she insisted, and with that, barged into the doctor's office and stood before his desk. "I want to know," she demanded. "Is he going to live or die?"

"Take it easy," the doctor said. "All he needs is three good meals every day and sex twice a day, and he'll be just fine."

When she reentered the waiting room where her husband was, he asked, "What did he say?"

"He said you're going to die," was her reply.

Humorous though it may be, whenever I tell it and people laugh, they also roll their eyes at their spouses with knowing looks.

Around my city we commonly see the "Newport Beach Phenomenon"—older men with younger women. More often than not, the man is some successful professional whose children left, wife is aging, and he divorces her to take up with a younger woman. His wife may have sacrificed to put him through school, slaved as his secretary when he started his business, devoted herself to rearing their children, and now when she can enjoy the fruit of her labor, he turns her out to fend for herself . . . while he prances around with younger women who satisfy his male ego. A man must understand that if a woman's loyalty can be bought, then it is no virtue and can be sold again to the highest bidder.

Later years are those when a ripened marriage can truly be "golden." Today I take more pleasure in my wife Nancy's pleasures than I do in my own. My tunnel vision concerning work leaves me little desire for anything else, so when I travel I almost never see the sights in the city where I'm going unless Nancy goes with me. Then I enjoy them through her as much as with her. It pleases me to see her pleasure. I enjoy making her happy. I know the value of the woman God allowed me to marry!

Nancy has proven her worth and value over the years of our marriage. I could never catalog all she has done for me—working to help support me in the early years, meticulous in housekeeping, faithfully stewarding the children through school and the maturing process, moving willingly with me at each new venture, watching the checkbook, forgiving my errors and sins, encouraging me in my failures, standing in the shadows when the spotlight of success fell on me, never missing a day reading the Bible or praying for her family, and really being the hub around which the wheel of the family turned. And now that she shows some signs of her age, needs a little more attention and fewer demands, I should begin to look for a new model? How absolutely asinine! Nancy has *increased* in value over the years. These are my years to give back to her some of what she has poured into my life. It's called gratitude; it's an element of love.

Others without a value system given them from the life of Christ and His Word dishonor God though they may be religious in practice. Of this sort are preachers whose attitude toward their parishioners is that they are just "tithers" and have no real value as persons. Such commercial preachers have existed from time immemorial. "By covetousness they will exploit you with deceptive words" is how Peter wrote about them (2 Peter 2:3). The prophet Jeremiah said they "prophesy lies" in the Lord's name (Jer. 23:25). Their ways are pernicious, noxious, and even fatal. Avoid them!

"The good shepherd gives His life for the sheep" (John 10:11). As Christ Himself was willing to do what was necessary for those God loved, so true shepherd-preachers lay down their lives for their flocks. Thank the Lord for godly pastors!

MONEY CLARIFIES YOUR VALUES

Money gives the appearance of worth. The more we pay for something, the greater the respect we show. Cars, homes, antiques, jewelry are given value through the money we spend on them. You get what you pay for. And we tend to invest our money in the things we value the most.

Many men establish their own worth or value by the esteem in which they hold themselves. Though some may esteem themselves too highly, others not enough, we must recognize our worth in terms of both money and respect.

Working in the warehouse at five dollars per hour and envying the man behind the glass barrier upstairs in his shirt and tie making fifty dollars per hour will not change your worth. "To increase in value, work on yourself," I heard a great man say. Education is a life-long process, not just for teen-time. You are never too old to learn, only too lazy to try.

There is truly an enigma concerning money and the gospel.

Church members admit that their ministers handle the words of eternal life well, but are content to leave them as nearly the lowest paid of all professions. Pastors are worthy of double honor (1 Tim. 5:17). Godly pastors are more valuable than governors or presidents because they watch after your soul's health.

For the first few years of our ministry to men, we subsisted on the free will offerings of attendees. That all changed when a principle of the kingdom of God sprang alive to me.

Jesus said, "Where your treasure is, there your heart will be also" (Luke 12:34).

Realizing that when people invest money into something they are going to be far more interested than mere spectators, we instituted a registration fee for our events. Men now stay for the entire event and attend even when the weather is atrocious. That paid registration fee became a treasure invested, so they put their hearts into the meeting.

That principle also teaches you that you can't build a church on people who don't tithe or invest financially in the church. Without the investment, they don't have their hearts in it. Their affection will follow their profits. If the church is without profit to them, they have no love for it. Duty will not keep them there when adversity comes.

It is so easy to be seduced by the culture around us, to embrace its values, and lose sight of the God-called life. The world believes that the Church should be poor and beggarly, without financial stability to advance the cause of Christ and that preachers should minister with a paltry income. To adopt that attitude is to allow the world to set standards for God's work.

Unregenerate men do not value the Church or gospel, so why should Christians regard their advice on finances? Without the "birthright" of Jesus Christ, they have no interest in the Church.

WHOEVER DICTATES YOUR VALUES BECOMES YOUR GOD

Your value system is usually created by God, you, or others—corporations, philosophies, religions, prophets, or parents.

Corporations dictate employees' value systems by wanting them to serve the corporation above God, family, or self. The call to worship the corporate logo with sacrifice is not uncommon today.

False prophets, gurus, vain philosophers, and wolves in sheep's clothing become gods to their followers who worship in slavish devotion. Satan's "messianic complex," in which he did not want to lead worship but be worshiped, is the core of cults and false religions.

Communism, rooted in atheistic anger, became the deity of two generations of people. Marx and Lenin became the prophets of the new religion. But communism was predicated on a lie, now obvious by its failure and collapse. Meanwhile, the gospel of Jesus Christ, so hated, ridiculed, and denied as the "people's opiate," is being eagerly embraced, not as narcotic, but as a cure, immunizing them against the toxin of tyranny.

Collective value systems are comprised of those of individuals. When a man claims his value system is his own, that he will live and die by it, he becomes his own Messiah. His counterfeit "trinity" is "me, myself, and I." Refusing to accept Christ, the true Messiah, a man comes short of the glory of God and will suffer the consequences for eternity. As his family's messiah he will answer for his idolatry when he stands before God.

INDIVIDUAL RIGHTS CANNOT EXCEED THE CORPORATE GOOD

The body's appendix, demanding for itself the vitality meant to give life to the entire body and expending it on itself, is an organ that often must be removed for the sake of the health of the body. Allowing one member of the body to usurp the functions of all is deadly.

Around the world AIDS activists can be anarchists in their insurrection, demanding that the moral men of society pay for the ills of the immoral. Dictators in their lusts rape the country to satisfy themselves, making their individual pleasure more important than the prosperity of the people.

Though still theologically debated, the apostle Paul's warning to women not to speak out in church was an application of this very principle. Their exercise of free speech disturbed the meeting, distracted the speaker, and put the entire meeting in disarray. Paul's injunction was never meant to be a muzzle on a woman's gifts, just her inadvertent utterance.

The value of the whole exceeds the value of the one.

Doctors major in health, not disease. The only reason they diagnose a disease is to find a cure. There is no cure needed without a disease. Surgery of the diseased appendix is necessary for the body to live. "Cutting out" the unsound is sound.

For the same reason, the apostle Paul advised the Corinthian church to set aside the immorally incestuous members. "A little leaven leavens the whole lump" (1 Cor. 5:6; Gal. 5:9). By giving the "brother" the benefits of membership in the church there was no need for repentance of the sin in his life (1 Cor. 5:11). By excising him, requiring repentance for readmission, the fear of the Lord would bring him to the place of repentance and restoration.

Recently I had a cutback in my staff. I never went through such agony before, the decision was so difficult, but it was necessary for the ministry to survive. Cutbacks in business in recession times are not because employers don't like employees, but because the survival of the business is at stake, and it has priority over the individual.

Not long ago, a union went on strike against a major corporation, and continued the strike until the corporation went out of business. Then, when the union members lost their jobs, they blamed the company. They were insisting on their individual rights—and they got them—the right to do anything they wanted once they lost their jobs. This is not to discount people's desires or needs for respect as individuals; nor to give license for immoral men to lord it over employees and treat them as chattel; but to give a principle by which we are to be guided in our values to work for the common good of all.

FATHERS PROVIDE THE FAMILY'S VALUE SYSTEM

Fathers provide the atmosphere in the home, whether present or absent. A father's responsibility is not to make his son's decisions, but to let his son see him make his. Children learn theory at school, but how to live at home.

As a boy, my mother took me to church faithfully, but my dad never attended. He loved pleasure, the fellowship of other men, recreation and sports, gambling, drinking, and so I left the church and followed Dad's path. Fortunately I could not outrun my mother's prayers, so for almost the last half-century, it has been my joy to serve the Lord.

The attack on the family that has increased in intensity in recent years has occupied the attention of ministers, but they have largely failed to correct the condition. The biblical pattern for the discipling of the family is this: The pastor disciples the man and the man disciples the family. However, for two generations pastors have taught men to bring their families to church and they will take the responsibility to disciple the family, through Sunday school, youth programs, ladies' Bible studies, and other assorted activities. In so doing the pastor becomes the surrogate father to every member of every family who attends the church. That is a burden too heavy for any one man to bear.

The greatest value of a father's legacy is in the faith he leaves in his child's life. His child's greatest treasure is his faith in God. It is of such value that it is invaluable.

VALUES CAN BE HELD, THEN DISCARDED

Some of the saddest words ever written about any man are those written in Scripture regarding a man called Demas. "Demas hath forsaken me, having loved this present world," Paul wrote of his former co-laborer (2 Tim. 4:10 KJV). Failing to esteem the reproach of Christ of greater riches than the pleasures of this world, Demas turned his back on the gospel and returned to his love of the world.

Did you ever see a dog vomit, then return and eat it? That's how Peter wrote about a man rejecting Christ and returning to his life of pleasure and sin (2 Peter 2:22).

In a meeting in Philadelphia, a gentleman who looked as if he were an executive or successful salesman, cornered me in the hallway. "I just wanted to tell you what happened to me today. My company gave me my bonus check, it was much larger than I thought it would be, and because it was enough money to buy some 'white powder,' I thought of doing it and celebrating my good fortune. Then I remembered about the dog and the vomit and the taste went out of it. Thanks for showing me that the old things are so putrid."

Don't discard the most valuable gift imaginable, the gift of salvation and friendship with God, for a few moments of ethereal and ephemeral pleasure with those who are wasting their lives. What value is there in that?

Every day, in every way, thank God for the gift of life, appreciate its value, cause it to increase in your life, and above all else give praise to the God of heaven who considered you valuable enough to pay the price for your eternal life. Your true value is in the value in which God holds you. That's eternal worth.

EVERYTHING IN LIFE HAS VALUE

Everything in life has value: actual, perceived, accrued. Some things are taken for granted and their value goes unappreciated until they are lost, stolen, or simply gone. One of them is time—so intangible, so valuable, so ill-treated, so bad when there is no more.

Time has intrinsic value.

Time wasted is lost.

Time spent is gone.

Time invested is multiplied.

When money or health diminish they can often be regained, but not time. Once time has gone by, it can only be recalled or regained in memory not in actuality.

Timing is the essential ingredient in success—being the right man at the right time in the right place. It's possible to be the right man at the right place but not at the right time and fail. Many mediocre men make a great success because they have come to the fore at the right time.

Influence has value. Leaders determine to influence; followers happen to influence. Using influence is wise. Selling it can be a criminal act. Companies pay advertising firms billions to influence people for their product.

Every man has influence. How you use it determines its value. Jesus used His influence to call people to God. His influence on people's lives is felt in every corner of the world, and His influence through people benefits society. The influence from the baptism of the Spirit with power is for the benefit of all mankind. The manifestations and gifts of the Spirit are to witness to the gospel of Jesus Christ, but when used only for personal benefit it is immoral.

There is even value in failure. Yesterday's dung is tomorrow's fertilizer. One man's junk is another man's antique. What seemed worthless yesterday may have great value tomorrow. Never throw away your failures; use them as the underpinning for right decisions today and tomorrow.

What is the stigma of Christianity to some is the glory of the cross to others.

The Bible lays out very clearly the value system God has for this world and us as persons. He valued us enough to send Christ to die for us. When we reject that basic truth we call God a liar (1 John 5:10). What makes a man think that after spending a lifetime rejecting God's Word, calling God a liar, aligning himself with God's enemies, that when he dies God is going to receive him gladly into heaven?

God establishes the value systems for the Church and the individual, and God is no pauper. God's throne and tabernacle in heaven are without peer. Nothing can compare with His glory. All the majesty of all the royalty that ever existed on earth combined cannot compare with a scintilla of the glory of God.

Eternal values in life are established by God through Jesus Christ.

To become a real man is to have real values.

Chapter 8

Maximizing Your Resources

The Sudan in Africa is a land under siege. Elements and people have both taken their toll. The Sudan had a famine that took the lives of 250,000 people in 1988. Civil war had wiped out 500,000 natives over the previous six years. Many of those annihilated were a tribe of giants called the Dinka, most of whom stand six feet tall and whose chiefs are always over seven feet. The Dinka are a warrior people who place great emphasis and pride on such things as courage and physical stature. Dinka males often bear scars from wounds suffered in spear and club fights. Among the Dinka, theft is almost nonexistent. A Dinka's word is his bond.

When asked by a reporter what it means to be a Dinka, the chief replied, "It means that one must be a husband to all people. It means one must protect others, provide for others, but always be ready to step in and decide what is right and wrong. A Dinka must be strong. He must be a man among men."[1]

Being a man in almost every culture means being ready to direct, protect, and correct. The three elements stem from God's instruction to Adam to guide, guard, and govern (Gen. 2:15). Many cultures subject boys to bloody rites of passage. Besides the shedding of blood, almost all include imperviousness to pain, exemplary courage in the face of danger, and the unflinching resistance to all threats to his manhood. Tears, softness, or weakness disqualify manliness.

Anthropologist David Gilmore, in his book *Manhood in the Making: Cultural Concepts of Masculinity,* writes,

> In East Africa young boys from cattle-herding tribes . . . are taken away from their mothers and subjected to painful circumcision rites by which they become men. If the Samburu boy cries out

while his flesh is being cut, if he so much as blinks an eye, he is shamed for life as unworthy of manhood. The Amhara, an Ethiopian tribe, have a passionate belief in masculinity called "wand-nat." To show their "wand-nat," Amhara youths are forced to engage in bloody whipping contests.[2]

Mr. Gilmore cites other bloody ordeals. In Melanesia, young boys are torn from their mothers and forced to undergo whipping, blood-letting, and beating, all of which the boys must endure stoically. The boys of the Tewa in New Mexico are taken away and lashed on the back with a crude yucca whip that draws blood and leaves permanent scars. "You are made a man," the elders tell them afterward. The aboriginal Mehinaku of Brazil scorn as effeminate those who are "stingy, weak, or impotent," according to Gilmore.

In America baseball and football are rites of passage. Some fathers consider "making the team" almost a matter of life and death. The intensity with which some dads pressure their sons into emotional stress beyond their years is appalling. These men are not aborigines, just American men, but with the same propensities as the unlearned, and whose games may not be with sticks and stones, but even more lethal with modern equipment. Baseball, football, basketball are often violent. There isn't much difference among men after all, just various methods of accomplishing the same maturation process.

Mr. Gilmore stated,

I've discovered there is almost a generic criterion of manhood across diverse societies. Manhood is based on being competent in three things: The first is provisioning. A real man provides for his wife, his children, and his group. . . . protection . . . Defending your clan or country is exclusively a male duty. . . . impregnating . . . In many cultures having lots of children and wives or mistresses shows that you're a real man.[3]

Gilmore concludes,

"Real men" are those who give more than they take, who . . . serve others by being brave and protective. . . . Real men do nurture. They do this by shedding their blood, their sweat, their semen; by bringing home food, producing children, or dying if necessary in far away places to provide security for their families. But this masculine nurturing is paradoxical. To be supportive, a man must first be tough in order to ward off enemies; to be generous, he must first be selfish in order to amass goods; to be tender, he must be aggressive enough to court, seduce, "win" a wife.[4]

In his research he found the commonality among men is to provide their blood, sweat, and semen for their progeny. Men are to be givers, surrendering themselves, even to extreme suffering, for the single purpose of providing for their clan, household, or family.

But a man (or a woman, for that matter) cannot provide what he does not possess. He can't give his wife a necklace if he doesn't have it—or the means to get it. He can't empathize with his wife or children if he lacks love or compassion. A man must first possess what he desires to give. Otherwise, his desire will go unfulfilled.

It's also true, however, that we do not own what we possess. We hold our possessions only for a season. Fame is fleeting. Money comes and goes. Friendships grow and falter. Mates walk beside us, but eventually die. Our possessions are not ours to keep, but rather ours to nurture and protect. We're called to be good stewards of what we have, whether it be our minds or bodies, our talents or dreams, our friendships or marriages . . . whatever.

Primitive societies have often understood this truth better than we have, particularly regarding the environment. The great environmental concern in our world today is an effort to rectify the damage done to earth by our poor stewardship of its resources. Around the world waters are polluted, rain forests are depleted, animals and fish are more scarce, and some so rare they are "endangered species" with legally sanctioned protection against further decimation. Many are concerned with the depletion of the ozone layer, citing the earth's warming trend as a warning, and declaring that unless we do something we face the extinction of man . . . all due to modern man's poor stewardship of God's creation.

Why? Because humans are basically selfish. We take and take and take, but give little or nothing in return. Humans have been this way since the first sin.

Our stewardship of the environment is akin to rape. We use and abuse it, then throw it away. Owners of factories spewing millions of gallons of sewage into lakes and streams, creating a scourge of diseases, when reprimanded and told to stop, spend millions in legal fees to maintain their right to pollute. We behave worse than animals.

When we care only for food and sex, prey upon one another, wander aimlessly through life seeking only personal pleasure, live by our instincts, we really do live on an animal level. But even animals don't destroy their habitat as we do. Nor do animals contaminate and pollute mentally, physically, and socially as we do. It was the assessment of man's parallel practices to that of animals that gave birth to theories that man descended from primates. Pastor Joseph Ripley said it best: "God didn't model man from a monkey, but men make monkeys of themselves."

The other day at the beach, I commended a city worker who was cleaning the rest areas after a holiday weekend, thanking him for what he was doing to maintain a nice place for us. Noting the great amount of trash, the indecent manner of littering, all the obscenities scrawled around, I commented to him, "Sometimes it seems that men act like animals."

With a voice of disdain that probably developed over weeks and months of dealing with the garbage, he said, "They are worse than animals."

Recently, after I conducted a men's seminar in an auditorium, the manager made a deliberate effort to speak to one of our staff members. "We want you to to have your next meeting here too. Your men were the best-behaved, cleanest, most courteous we have ever had here. We don't know about your religion, but we know about you. This place is yours any time you want it."

I couldn't help but contrast the statement of the maintenance worker at the beach with what the auditorium manager said. Jesus really does make a difference in people. Their natures show in their responsible stewardship.

Humanity, God's crowning creation—reduced by sin to the pitiful, pathetic polluters of the atmosphere of earth and soul. How far we have fallen, and how desperately we want to avoid responsibility for our actions. That old adage is still so right: "It takes a man to admit he's wrong."

The reason Christ came to redeem us from the curse of sin was to raise us from the depths of our depravity, give us a new nature with God's own power to be good stewards, and glorify God on the earth. The miracle of God's grace is that He gives us the power of His Spirit to enable us to live the Christ-life. We are stewards of that grace (1 Peter 4:10).

Humankind, through Adam, has the responsibility to be a steward and leader (Gen. 1:26). Jesus, the last Adam, fulfilled these responsibilities while on earth, where the first Adam had failed. "While I was with them in the world, I kept them in Your name," Jesus said to His Father when He prayed (John 17:12). Jesus was a good steward of the men who were with Him. So was King David with his four hundred men. But not King Saul. He exchanged the men God gave him for those of his choosing, and that was part of his undoing.

Remember, the kingdom of God does not run on sentiment; it runs on truth. Even those who maintain the faith, love God, and desire to fulfill His calling and keep His commandments can make miserable mistakes in their stewardship. "To whom much is given, from him much will be required" (Luke 12:48).

Ministers don't own the ministry they are in; they are only stewards of the grace God has given them. All true gospel ministry is that of the Lord Jesus Christ, and those called to preach are only stewards of His gospel. It is His Church, His Truth, His Word, His Spirit, His Commandments, His Blood, His Life. His stewards must be found faithful (1 Cor. 4:2).

William and Stan came to me to ask for some help. They were confused, hurt, and discouraged by what was happening to their ministerial organization. For years it had been a force for good throughout the world, but in recent years members had become disgruntled with the leadership, disaffected by its methods, and disturbed by the rapid decrease in influence and membership.

An attempt by some members to unseat the president went so far as to legally challenge the powers of his office. The resultant discord even divided close friends such as William and Stan.

The entire conflict and ultimate loss might have been avoided except for the truculence of its leader. Because he had helped found the organization, had been its only leader over the years, he had become possessive, as if he were an owner, not a steward. Many of his associates had grown in ministry with him, and there was a close affinity among them all.

Scripture says, "Better is a poor and wise youth / Than an old and foolish king who will be admonished no more" (Eccl. 4:13).

Aging has great benefits, but when men grow old in their position, set in their ways, and the time comes to leave, they may choose to leave peacefully and gracefully or contentiously. Much of what happens has to do with how they regard their position and power. Being a founder and owner of the company can be deceptive when a person's ego becomes involved possessively and wants to maintain control, though he is no longer mentally sharp and professionally aggressive. Though he owns the company, he is still only a steward, and a good steward concerned for the welfare of something he devoted much of his life to must know when to step down and let another carry on the work, trusting the capabilities of a successor. In this case the visionary-leader refused to admit it was time for him to leave, he would not change, and the organization floundered.

In ministry, where God anoints and appoints, leaders must be careful in taking succession into their own hands. A classic illustration is in the life of King David who, though old and feeble, remained king. God removed his kingship upon his death, no sooner. When proud aides or seditious sons sought to overthrow David, God preserved him on the throne of Israel and destroyed the rebels. After Samuel anointed the boy David to be king, Saul had become enraged. He chased David for years, but David never retaliated. He had opportunities to kill Saul and ascend the throne a little ahead of schedule, but he never took them. He waited for God's timing. Though David committed adultery and murder in his lifetime, he was God's anointed king. He showed the king's enemies that when men seek to take God's place in dealing with His anointed leaders, they put themselves in personal jeopardy. God dealt with David in a way no man could ever conceive or carry out. God is a just God, and judgment must be left to His wisdom and mercy.

The story of a great computer company interested me. The president turned control of the company over to his son, only to lose hundreds of millions of dollars, and had to demote the son and take charge of the management again. The son did not inherit the father's ability or discernment, just his business. The Bible also records cases where children inherited fathers' businesses and blessings, but had to learn ability and discernment on their own.

Abraham's sons inherited his ministry and God's promises to him, by God's directive. A great lesson can be learned from Abraham's descendants, Isaac and Jacob. They each inherited the ministry of their father, but had to "dig the wells" as their father had before them (Gen. 26:15–33). Digging the wells typified the need for each son to do the works of his father to obtain the same qualifications for leadership. Each had to undertake his peculiar rite of passage. But this was not an earthly proving process they sought; it was a heavenly confirmation. Sons can inherit ministries, but they cannot inherit God's anointing.

Many ministries taken over by sons who lack their fathers' spirit expire from the lack of life-giving force given by the Spirit of God. Businesses suffer in the secular realm from successor sons who cannot carry on the father's vision, or because no men were well trained to succeed the leader, or by bringing in men from outside who have no concept of the vision, principles, or goals of the founder-visionary.

Those visionaries who launch their business ventures with few resources or little manpower must stock the store, take care of the books, watch the inventory—in other words do it all—guide, guard, and govern. As the business grows they can hire bookkeepers, supervisors, and eventually devote themselves to just guiding the growth. Though they may have others do the guarding and governing, they can never give away the authority to guide. Only one man is the visionary, and when he relinquishes his role to unprepared men, the business begins to fail. The visionary is the force behind the vision.

William Tyler Page wrote "The American's Creed" in 1917:

I believe in the United States of America as a government of the people, by the people, for the people, whose just powers are derived from the consent of the governed.[5]

The founding fathers of our nation did not want the power of government to be in the hands of an established rulership such as the English monarchy America had just thrown off. The right to govern is in the hands of the citizenry, not those in the legislative, executive, or judicial branches of government.

Legislators were to be those elected from the ranks of the common citizen. Shopowners, teachers, housewives, bankers, and all other citizens were to be among those selected.

Today too many professional politicians, mostly lawyers, hold office too long and become entrenched in power. Legislators only have power by the consent of the governed. By default, unqualified or evil men hold office.

To have the power to vote and not do it is wickedness. In the parable of the talents Jesus said the servant who did nothing was wicked and slothful, insolent and indolent.

When moral men abandon the voting booth in a fatalistic attitude that says, "It won't do any good anyhow," they are being deceived. Those governed by dictatorial fiat but who have regained the right to vote, regard it as almost a sacred duty. Recognizing the responsibility to govern, by voting and monitoring those elected, is being a good steward. Poor stewardship of the polling place is bad citizenship.

God directly gave Adam the charge to guide, guard, and govern the earth and its reproductive process. When Eve and a family followed, Adam became a steward of his entire family with the same threefold responsibility: guide, guard, govern.

This translates into (Eph. 5:28–29): direct, protect, correct. Nourish, cherish, admonish.

In the triune nature of the Godhead, theologians have given us an understanding of the Father, Son, and Holy Spirit:

Son = the Visionary
Holy Spirit = the Administrator
Father = the Ruler

Man, in God's image, has the triune responsibility to be the: visionary, administrator, ruler.

When Christ came, He revealed Himself as: prophet, priest, and king.

Fathers are called to be prophet, priest, and king to their families. Prophets speak for God to the people; priests speak for the people to God; and kings are qualified to rule by their willingness to serve. Men are required to fill all three roles.

As Christ is to the Church, so a husband is to his wife, his family, his possessions, his job, and all else that God has given him. Man's stewardship can never be relinquished. Judgment of a man comes from the measure to which he succeeds as a steward.

A man's responsibility to his family is to direct, protect, and correct; nourish, cherish, admonish; to be the prophet, priest, and king. When a man accepts that assignment from God, the family structure falls into place. When he doesn't, the result is a family out of order, and even out of control.

A man's family is a reflection of his godly stewardship. It's the reason for God's requirement to assess a man's ability to lead his family as the proof of his ability to lead a church (1 Tim. 3:1–11). The family is the microcosm of the Church.

A man may succeed as a steward in business, but fail as an agent of God at home. The determination of his success or failure is not in what he takes but in what he gives. The more he serves, the greater he becomes. Jesus came not to be ministered to, but to minister.

Real men hold that same attitude.

Chapter 9
Staying on Top

As I drove into Los Angeles to minister at an inner city church, the area began to look familiar to me. A street sign caught my attention and suddenly I realized that I had lived on that street years before. Quickly redirecting my car, I drove through the neighborhood and saw the house I had lived in as a boy. I began to reflect on how many decades it had been since I lived there.

Driving home after the meeting I began to reminisce about my life. I had not thought about some of those events, places, or things in years. Boyhood in Los Angeles, the Coast Guard, marrying Nancy, salvation, the pastorate, the mission field. Some of it almost seemed like a former life. My reverie brought me to the present joy and fulfillment I have with a ministry to men, and how God's Word had continued to change my life to bring me to this day. I meditated for a moment on the specific words that changed the direction of my ministry, and therefore, my career.

In 1974 Joy Dawson was teaching a series on intercessory prayer at the church we pastored. It was her teaching on the "Nine Principles of Intercession" that changed my and Nancy's marriage. Joy taught us that prayer produces intimacy, and our prayer time together began to produce vulnerability and affection that changed our marriage. For that I am eternally grateful to Joy, but there was more.

One beautiful afternoon during her stay, an associate pastor and I decided to escape to the golf course for a quick nine. Joy wanted to go with us. That afternoon she was an irrepressible free spirit— barefooted, running, skipping, laughing, and proving she could still do back flips. Then suddenly, just as I was lining up a putt she said, "I've got a word for you, Ed. You can be one of God's thousands of disappointments, or one of His few successes. To succeed you will need a higher degree of holiness, and a far better understanding of intercession." I missed the putt, but got the point.

At the sound of her words there was an immediate awareness that this was divinely inspired. Taking it to heart, Nancy and I accepted the challenge and began to practice the nine steps in intercessory prayer Joy taught. The results were revolutionary.

Years later, the Lord impressed me again with His Word. At the time I was fasting and walking the beach daily in the cool, foggy predawn hours. As I cried out to God all alone, His Spirit spoke to my spirit five "words." They were:

"Sanctify yourself."

"Preach the Word."

"Go doubting nothing."

"Use the gold, but don't touch the glory."

"Pray this prayer: Acts 4:24."

Five years later, George Otis attended a dinner meeting where I was enlisting sponsors for a new ministry to men. During his message he suddenly stated, "This ministry is running late."

I realized this was a statement that I should regard sacredly and obediently. I resigned the church and every organization I was working with within twenty-four hours, and forty-eight hours later I was launching full-time into a ministry to men from my garage.

In late 1979, one morning at the breakfast table in my home, as I was relating the text of my initial message to men to my wife and daughter, commenting on the problem of sex sins in society and the religious community, my daughter, Joann, said, "Dad, don't you know sex sins will be the problem of the Church in the eighties?"

On the first weekend of February 1980, at a men's retreat in Oregon, I made that statement. I did not realize how prophetic it was. By the end of the decade newspaper headlines flaunted the sexual dalliances of ministers, church leaders, and distraught ministers and congregations faced the dilemma of discipline, forgiveness, and restoration in grace and love for those involved. The 1980s are called the "Decade of Greed." Greed is a manifestation of lust.

God speaks in various ways at various times. For example, He speaks through:

- *His Word*. (Matt. 4:4; Deut. 8:3) God speaks to us from His Word, the Bible. That is the rule, not the exception, so daily reading of the Word is vital.

- *An audible Voice.* (Matt. 3:17, 17:5; Acts 9:3–5) This is a special means by which God communicates with man, such as He did with Moses through a burning bush, Christ's baptism in the Jordan, or Saul on the Damascus road. This is the exception, not the rule.
- *Angels.* (Judges 6:12; Matt. 1:20) God sends these messengers with announcements, counsel, warning, and exhortations.
- *Dreams.* (Gen. 37:5; Matt. 1:20) Dreams accompanied by a specific interpretation provide energy for ministry fulfillment.
- *Visions.* (Acts 10:10, 26:19; Rev. 1:9–20) God speaks through visual manifestations, as He did to John on the Island of Patmos, to Peter about ministering to the Gentiles, and to Paul about going to Macedonia.
- *Spirit to spirit.* (Luke 2:26; Acts 22:23; Rom. 8:14–16) God's Spirit witnesses to man's spirit in saving grace whereby we say, "Abba, Father." To be "led by the Spirit" is an evidence of our sonship to God. Our spirits also bear witness to God's and to each other's.
- *Prophets.* (Luke 1:67–70; Eph. 2:19–22; Heb. 1:1) Foundational revelation came through apostles and prophets. We are to take heed to the prophets, but beware of the false prophet!
- *Godly counsel.* (Acts 5:34; Prov. 11:14) For example, Gamaliel's counsel from the Lord spared God's people. Solomon recognized the value of others' input too.
- *Gifts of the Spirit.* First Corinthians 12 lists the gifts of the Spirit, and the Book of Acts shows each gift working in believers' lives.
- *Circumstances.* Positive or negative, God can use them to confirm His Word in your life.
- *Desires of the heart.* (Ps. 37:4) When we are "born again" and become "new creatures," God gives us a new nature (2 Peter 1:4). Old things pass away, and all becomes new (2 Cor. 5:17). As God transforms our hearts, He places desires and dreams within us that will guide our lives, as He did with Joseph (Gen. 37).

These various avenues through which God leads us are a way of life to be sought after by those desiring to become real men. If God wants to bring His message to a police station, hospital, or construction site and you are there—you become God's revelation to those people. Just as Jesus was God's revelation of God on earth, so men stand in Christ's stead as God's revelation to others. What you do when God speaks to you affects you, those around you, and hundreds of lives beyond.

Through the years, God in His faithfulness, has continually led Nancy and me. By hearing His voice through those ways in which only God can communicate, our lives changed slowly into what we are today. God's "word" did not stop at our doorsteps, but became something greater in life as we continued to submit to Him, and today the Christian Men's Network is reaching men throughout the world.

"He sent His word and healed them," the Bible says (Ps. 107:20). God's large-scope pattern is: God sends a word, gives it a body, and brings healing to the world.

- The life of Jesus Christ illustrates the pattern. Jesus came as the "Word," assumed a flesh-and-blood body, and brought the healing message of grace and redemption to the world (John 1:1, 14; Mal. 4:2).
- God gave the gospel message to the disciples, who became the Body of Christ, and brought healing throughout the known world.

Did you notice that all God's work begins with His Word? His Word launched creation and continues to precede His work, even to this day (Gen. 1:1–3; John 1:1).

- God sent His Word to meet the critical needs of society and bring the Dark Ages to an end. God needed men to know He saved them not by works, indulgences, or priestly pardon, but by grace through faith. Faith, not works, justified them. So God gave the word *justification* (Hab. 2:4; Rom. 1:17) to Martin Luther. Those who believed it and followed Luther became "Lutherans," and they brought healing balm to the world.
- Another need arose and God gave the word *sanctification* (1 Thess. 5:23) to John Wesley. The people who followed Wesley and his methodical life-style became known as "Methodists," and they brought the healing message of sanctification to their generation.
- The word that sparked the Holiness movement was *separation* (2 Cor. 6:17).
- *Power* (Acts 1:8) came to the Pentecostals.
- *Renewal* (Rom. 12:12) to the Charismatics.

Each "word" developed a body of believers and brought healing to all who trusted in the Lord (1 Thess. 2:13). Each revelation was important because it changed the course of Church history, which in turn influenced the destiny of generations.

Immediately following the word, the pattern of revelation and the process of crystallization begins. Nothing is wrong with any true word from the Lord, but everything is wrong with the crystallization of it. The degenerative trap of crystallization is what ensnares most people and denominations, and it is often the culprit when marriages and businesses fail.

Learn this well: It is easier to obtain than to maintain.

The corollary to this principle is the pattern of revelation and the process of crystallization.

The pattern and process are: Revelation—Inspiration—Formalization—Institutionalization—Crystallization—Secularization.

THE PROGRESSION

Revelation. Understanding God's Word always comes by way of revelation. God does not explain Himself, He reveals Himself. In His own Book, He starts out, "In the beginning, God . . ." (Gen. 1:1). Revelation becomes alive in the heart and brings light and understanding. Revelation about God Himself brings a fresh flow of spiritual expression, including new patterns of worship and music. New wine is not put in old wineskins (Matt. 9:17).

Inspiration. Inspiration is the result of revelation. Revelation inspires change through the "expulsive power of a new affection." A dead leaf from winter drops off when spring comes and the sap begins to flow through the tree. Likewise, when inspiration rises within us, the fresh affection drives out the old and brings in the new. Old habits drop off and new habits are formed. Aspirations are heightened, behaviors are created, modified or removed, plans are reformulated, ideals are restated.

Formalization. The changes brought by inspiration are developed, codified, and formalized. A desire comes for acceptance and association with those who have received similar revelation and share common goals and purpose. In the Church, denominations arise with doctrines, tenets of faith, and standardization of beliefs to be passed on to the next generation. In relationships, distance is measured by formality, intimacy is measured by informality. The more formal the application the more distant the worshiper to the initial experience.

At this critical point of development, men must return to the Lord for fresh revelation. A new "word" will incorporate new inspiration and stave off the degenerative tendency.

Institutionalization. Over time, formalization will evolve into institutionalization. Men begin to go through the motions without emotions. Doctrines and creeds congeal, and desires arise to maintain the status quo. It is here where, if new revelation is not sought and embraced, which in turn produces progress, then technical and mechanical procedures set in and men commit to maintaining the status quo of the initial thrust. It is also where dull, uninspired life begins, and the political replaces the prophetic.

Crystallization. The result of institutionalization is crystallization. Areas of life outside the formalized structure are truncated. New revelation is not integrated because of a hardened, unresponsive, and negative attitude. Prejudice and faultfinding intensifies and the syndrome of cynicism begins. "Crystallites" become stumbling blocks to others.

Secularization. Crystallization leads to secularization. Secularization is the return to what existed before the initial revelation. It's the end of a process that begins so wonderfully and powerfully, and winds up so pitiably and miserably.

No better illustration can be given than to encourage a look at the marvelous university campuses, established by godly men of faith for the fundamental purpose of educating their youth and preparing them for a life of Christian service in proclaiming the truths of Christ. Today, so many of them are secular institutions staffed by mockers, skeptics, and antagonists to the Christian faith. What started with a pattern of revelation ends by the process of crystallization, terminating in secularization.

Men determine the process of crystallization by rejecting fresh revelation. God is not stagnant. He is constantly revealing Himself in accomplishing the restitution of all things before the second coming of Christ. How pathetic to see men who have crystallized on God! They are critical and hardened in attitudes, ways, and habits. Passion is the sin of youth, pride the sin of middle age, and prejudice the sin of old age. Prejudiced and crystallized, having lost the joy of salvation and left their first love, the only mode of assuaging their guilt is by self-justification, which issues in an effort to ridicule the fresh wave of God's Spirit and revelation.

If crystallized men are unwilling to bend or bow, their only hope is to be broken so God can mend them. Better to humble themselves, repent, and ask God for fresh revelation, the restoration of His joy, and the vitality of true relationship with Him.

It's easy to picture the religious pattern and process in colleges and denominations, but the pattern and process is derived from individuals. It occurs in marriages, families, churches, businesses, and even nations can fall subject to the process of crystallization.

Let me give you another illustration of this.

In marriage the process can take this form:

Revelation: "She's the one!" The new life of love within you sparks an awareness of beauty, music, and perhaps poetry. You hear birds, smell flowers, rediscover the joy of taking walks.

Inspiration: "Will you marry me?" The feeling of belonging together is overwhelming. In the wake of fresh romance you forget old affections.

Formalization: "I do." You take the vows, create priorities for your lives, and set your course together.

Institutionalization: "You take me for granted." Failing to recapture or renew revelation and inspiration, formalized lives become like machinery grinding along, often with friction, without fresh oil. The oil of discovery, finding something new to appreciate, another gift or grace found, is the essence of revelation in marriage. When the institution of marriage overtakes the inspiration of romance, crystallization is setting in.

Crystallization: "It's too late for us." Judgmental, faultfinding, unresponsive attitudes toward each other fill the vacuum left by the loss of revelation and inspiration.

Secularization: Divorce.

My advice to men the world over has been to tell their wives every day that they love them. Go on a honeymoon at least once every six months—*more* often if you have children at home! (This can be as simple as a night in a local motel or a friend's vacated house; leave the kids with the neighbors!) Turn to your wife *today*, look her straight in the eyes, and say, "You are God's gift to me, and I love you." Pray for her and with her. Prayer produces intimacy.

The other day I looked in my closet and all my clothes were freshly laundered and put away. It occurred to me I had not appreciated that faithful loving service, but over the years had begun to take it for granted. That was a revelation. I thanked Nancy, bought her a gift of appreciation, and told her how precious she was to do that for me. It provided her with a word of inspiration. So often it is the little things that we take for granted that are the basis for a fresh word of gratitude and appreciation. See the attraction it inspires when you begin to confess your love. An old marriage can restore youth to the spouses when both walk in fresh inspiration.

My friend Arnie has spent time with me in meetings, traveling, and worshiping. His marriage had institutionalized but he blamed his wife for the poor relationship. Then he reread my book *Maximized Manhood* and realized he had begun to take his wife for granted. After changing his attitude and approach toward his wife and marriage he told me, "Ed, I began to treat her every day like I was courting her. When I did, I discovered new things about her I liked, and she began to appeal to me in the same way she did when we first met."

Without going back to find fresh revelation of her, Arnie's path was the same as countless others leading him to crystallization and divorce. Fresh revelation brought new inspiration.

In business, the process can take this form:

Revelation: "I can do it!" An idea springs up to do something better and cheaper than anyone has done before.

Inspiration: "Let's get started." Research, a business plan, and investment follow as the new business gets underway.

Formalization: "We did it!" With the moving of the first units and the hiring of employees, patterns and procedures develop. A sales network materializes and profits begin to come in.

Institutionalization: "We've never done it that way before." New ideas and a fresh approach meet with resistance. Opportunities are not even noticed because of concentration on the routine. The product line stagnates and sales level off. The company is comfortable in what it has accomplished and doesn't respond to current trends or innovation.

Crystallization: "They'll never do it." Competition arises utilizing ideas and innovations, but the crystallized company watches with cynicism. Faultfinding brings lawsuits that fight competitors to ensure they cannot take over the market. The company is dying but refuses to acknowledge it.

Secularization: Bankruptcy or a hostile takeover.

Married, in business, employed, or simply living—you need fresh revelation. You need to be inspired to greatness. The lesson is this: If you settle for old revelation without ever finding new and fresh, your inspiration will stagnate, harden into a rigid form of institutionalization—and you will crystallize. Crystallization can occur mentally, socially, educationally, politically, religiously, and so on.

When the Israelites crossed the Jordan River, Joshua piled stones from the middle of the river, and told the men with him the pile was for the benefit of future generations, when they would ask, "What do these stones mean?" Then the parents would give their sons and daughters the understanding of how they came into the Promised Land by the supernatural power of God. Young people would learn from them about the presence and power of God (Josh. 4:4–9). Each new generation would then be inspired to seek the same supernatural power in the presence of their Jehovah God.

God is a God of perpetuity. He wanted each succeeding generation to experience Him personally and know His grace and power in their lives. However, those who crossed the Jordan forgot to tell the younger, and the younger didn't ask. The outcome of neglect was lamentably expressed in a terse statement in Scripture: "Another generation arose after them who did not know the LORD" (Judg. 2:10).

Cathedrals, churches, universities serve as reminders of a "word" from the Lord, testimonies to His supernatural power in bringing the forbears out of spiritual darkness into light, but now have lost their meaning through crystallization. Denominations and political organizations especially have strayed progressively from their founding virtues over time. As a result, much of our world has changed from God-fearing to God-ignorant.

A Gallup Poll suggests that, while religion is growing in importance in the United States, morality is losing ground. How can this be? Maybe because, as George Gallup points out, "The vast majority of us say that religion is important in our lives, but not the *most* important influence." Surface interest and involvement are high, but deep commitment is low.

"We venerate the Bible, but do not read it," Gallup said. "Few Christians say they are making a truly earnest effort to follow the example of Jesus Christ," and only twelve percent fall into a category of "highly spiritually committed."[1]

In the zeal of a conversion experience, or the thrill of a spiritual victory, we must not forget to go back to God to find fresh revelation again. The Israelites had to have fresh manna daily (Exod. 16:16–

21)—otherwise it would grow stale and lifeless. If we try to satisfy ourselves only with original revelation, and not discover God anew, we will eventually deteriorate into mediocrity, or worse. When that happens, Bible reading is reduced to quoting songbooks; prayer is modified to sermonizing to God; faith is diminished to presumption.

There is a fine line between faith and presumption. There is a great difference between God doing the work through us and us doing the work through God. Letting God be "the Lord of the work," instead of our doing "the work of the Lord" is how one Christian author put it.[2] Jesus Christ did not give you a backbone. He *is* your backbone.

"Without Me you can do nothing," Jesus said (John 15:5). Powerful claim. Powerful truth.

At the battle of Jericho, the Israelites had moved with faith and power and were victorious. Then, relying on experience to carry them, they went to Ai and were soundly defeated (Josh. 6–7). The problem: In their self-sufficiency they failed to pray. Forgetting to seek God, they failed to act in faith.

Adam did the same after Eve's temptation. When she offered the fruit, he just didn't pray or ask God what to do (Gen. 3:6). The disciples were prayerless in the garden of Gethsemane (Luke 22:45), so Christ went to the cross alone.

Seeking God for more understanding and knowledge, obtaining His perspective on matters in our lives, finding wisdom and truth concerning the totality of our lives are endeavors of the real man. Being content to quote familiar Scripture is not a sign that new facets of God's character are being discovered and understood.

The Word says,

> "Eye has not seen, nor ear heard,
> Nor have entered into the heart of man
> The things which God has prepared for those who love Him."
> But God has revealed them to us through His Spirit. (1 Cor.
> 2:9–10)

God has revelation for you! God always meets the contemporary needs of a contemporary society with contemporary means. God never tires of revealing Himself to men, nor do real men tire of God.

Part 4

Real Heart

■ ■ ■

Chapter 10

The Cornerstone of Character

On a Christian television program broadcast, the host and I were discussing the subject of faithful men when he asked me point-blank, "What if a faithful man is unfaithful, what then?"

My answer was just as straightforward.

"When a faithful man is unfaithful, he is faithful to repent!"

We are all flawed. And when we discover perfection, we have a tendency to crucify it. Just ask Jesus about that.

"Commit these to faithful men who will be able to teach others also" (2 Tim. 2:2) is the principle of discipleship. The common error of transposition perverts that to: "Commit to able men who shall be faithful." God commits to character, not talent. That perversion is the basis for problems in business, church, and marriage.

When a woman marries a man of ability, talent, or dynamic personality, then discovers he is unfaithful, it will make her life a hell instead of a heaven. An employer hiring a man based solely on his resume can have his business ruined by the employee's unfaithfulness. It's common for employers, pastors—really any man—to be impressed with men of charisma, talent, ability, and as a result commit some aspect of management or church life to the man. Then they suffer the chaos and loss from his unfaithful practice.

Not only does Scripture affirm that God is faithful (Deut. 7:9), but it declares that Christ "was faithful to Him who appointed Him, as Moses also was faithful in all His house" (Heb. 3:2).

"He who is faithful in a very little thing, is faithful also in much; and he who is dishonest and unjust in a very little thing is dishonest and unjust also in much" (Luke 16:10 AB).

Faithfulness is the cornerstone of character.

Jesus' parables of the "talents" illustrated divine principles of faithfulness in daily life (Matt. 25:14–30; Luke 19:12–27). In the parable, a master gave an equal sum to three servants and went away. When he returned, two had invested theirs for greater returns, while one had hidden his in the ground, not even banking it to collect interest. The master gave the poor steward's sum to those who had increased their investments, plus more to reinvest.

In this parable, Jesus taught the "Law of Capital," or the "Law of Increase and Decline." Basically stated, by use you possess and increase, and by disuse you decline and lose. When a man with a nineteen-inch bicep, who can lift one hundred pounds off a table with one hand, places his arm in a sling for three months to keep from hurting it, he deceives himself to think he can then take the arm out of the sling and lift the same weight. By not using the arm, his strength declined and he lost the nineteen-inch bicep and the ability he once had. "Use it or lose it" is the colloquial way of saying it.

The principle works with faith, love, knowledge, money, talent, or whatever a person possesses. Learn the piano as a child, fail to continue to practice, and as an adult the talent is gone. Hide money away, and years later it will have lost much of its purchasing power.

Remember, we do not own what we possess, we are only the stewards of it. A good steward holds on to what he is given, and uses it or increases it. The key to increase is investment.

Look at what happened to the faithful stewards in the parable. Those who invested their talent were entrusted with more (Matt. 25:28–29). The reward for being trustworthy is greater trust.

The steward who buried his sum lost what he had and saw it given to another who had more. He was not a profligate, embezzler, or thief. His sin was not in what he did, but in what he did not do. He was penalized because he did nothing. It's the penalty of the negligent.

When brought to account by his master, rather than admit his failure, he charged the master with being cruel, unjust, and hard. The accusation was that the master enriched himself by others' toil, expected gain where he had not labored, expected to get something for nothing, and the steward justified himself at his master's expense (Matt. 25:24–26). Self-justification has been the error of humanity since Adam blamed Eve, and Eve blamed the devil.

The "do-nothing" steward's attitude was that returning the same sum should be sufficient cause for reward and recompense. The master's reply was that if he really felt that way, then out of fear rather than respect of the master, the steward should have made an investment and not just buried the sum.

Calling the steward wicked and slothful, the master removed him from service. The goodness of the steward became no good or "good-for-nothing." Indolence and insolence are often the characteristics of the unfaithful. Indolence in doing nothing, and insolence in passing blame on to others.

One author noted that "do nothing" men give the following reasons for their actions: they refuse to do anything if they can't do it all; they refuse to help if they are not allowed to lead; they refuse if they know there are others involved who could do better.

You build character as you would an altar or building. Block upon block, decision upon decision, line upon line, little upon little.

Jesus also said, "And if you have not been faithful in what is another man's, who will give you what is your own?" (Luke 16:12).

On the shelf over my desk is a newspaper clipping encased in plastic, bearing the headline: "Entrepreneurs name top 100 young tycoons." The average age of all of them is 26.8, and of the top ten entrepreneurs 30 or younger, managing companies with annual sales of $20 million or more, fourth on the list is Stephen King. Pizza Hut of Cincinnati was included as a part of the business group. It earned $52.3 million in 1987.

Stephen had disciplined himself for years to read the Bible daily, reading it through on a yearly basis. He not only read it, but studied it and applied the principles he learned to his life and business. Upon graduation from college, debating what direction his life would go and what his career direction would take, his stepfather asked Stephen to assume the management of a Pizza Hut he owned. Stephen agreed and assumed the management of a business that was deep in debt, had low employee morale, and was considered a loser. Applying himself to learn and master the business, Stephen set a specific agenda to educate himself, cut costs, and turn a profit.

Several years later, after the first business became profitable, another opportunity became available. Stephen approached his stepfather with a recommendation to invest in it also, and seven years later, they owned and managed dozens of restaurants. Since then, the successful operation has been sold for a profit.

By taking the principles Christ gave, applying it to his life, becoming "faithful in that which is another man's," Stephen qualified himself to have his own and is exercising his entrepreneurial skills successfully in his own businesses today. The teachings of Jesus are not just for Sunday morning ministry texts, but are the source of wisdom and life. The real reason more men do not realize more from life through the Scriptures is basically because they are "hearers" of the word, and not "doers" (James 1:22).

Even when they do not know the principle as Christ taught it, but live it, they succeed by it. I was riding with a pastor in Sacramento from the airport to the hotel. He was telling me of the increase in his congregation's attendance, the exciting plans for the new building they just moved into, how men volunteered their services for its completion, and how great it all was. Later in the conversation he told me that when he attended college, he was the head usher in a church. He said his service there had been a great maturation process that prepared him for ministry. During the two years he was there he never missed a Sunday, attended every session he possibly could, and learned so much while doing it all.

I looked at him and exclaimed, "Bill, don't you realize that you qualified yourself for the benefits you are receiving now by your faithfulness to that pastor? Because you were faithful in that which was another man's, you qualified yourself for what you are enjoying now."

After I taught this biblical principle at a gathering of men in Phoenix, one of them stood to tell me what the truth of the principle did for him.

"I am having trouble with my two daughters," he said. "There is nothing that I can think of that would cause their resentments. Today when I heard that principle, I realized I also have two stepdaughters, and I have not been faithful to them as I have to my own. I've been unfaithful to the daughters of another man. Now I know the source of my problem. When I get home I am going to become a faithful steward of my stepdaughters, and when I do I know God will restore my relationship to my own."

Another man stood and said, "For nine years I have been working for the same man, but for the last seven I have wanted my own business. I believe I can run a business better than he does, develop the business better, and could be more successful than he has been. Now, I realize why I don't have my own business. I have not been faithful in this man's business, so I've never qualified myself for my own. When I go back to work I am going to make him the best employee he ever had, see to it the business is profitable, and then I believe I'll be qualified to have my own!"

Think for a moment about how many men are being curtailed, hurt, denied prosperity, increase, and higher position, because of their unwillingness to be faithful in that which is another man's. Frustrated, hampered, and throttled in their desires, they fail to realize the necessity to prove faithful in that which is another man's trust, in order to qualify themselves to obtain their own desires.

Elisha qualified himself to receive Elijah's mantle by adhering to the principle of being faithful in that which is another man's. His faithfulness in serving qualified him for the oracle gift in Elijah's prophetic office (2 Kings 3:11). Joshua was faithful to Moses, and became qualified to lead Israel after Moses' death. It was critical that Joshua constantly and faithfully serve Moses to prove himself able to follow God's commands in leading the nation of Israel (Num. 27:18). His submission qualified him for the commission.

"Consider the Apostle and High Priest of our confession, Christ Jesus, who was faithful to Him who appointed Him, as Moses also was faithful in all His house" (Heb. 3:1–2). Scripture is emphatic in referring to Jesus Christ as *the* faithful One.

He was constant, loyal, and submitted to the work and will of His heavenly Father. There are at least three elemental ingredients in faithfulness: constancy, loyalty, and submission, all of which Jesus exhibited.

Constancy means steadfast, never varying, continually recurring. Christ Himself was constant in His application to the Father's will. He was loyal and submitted. He showed Himself to be the epitome of the faithful Man.

Loyalty is the state of being firmly attached to someone or something by affection, sympathy, self-interest, or commonality. Loyal men are not secret-tellers. Their confidentiality is uncompromising. They are quick to stand for the cause or person to which they are loyal.

Nehemiah was loyal to the vision of rebuilding the wall and temple of Jerusalem when the Israelites returned from captivity. The temple he risked his life to build, wielding a tool in one hand and a weapon in the other, was known as Zerubbabel's temple, but much of the credit goes to him and the loyal men with him. Nehemiah was in a place of leadership and, like earlier governors, had the opportunity to place a heavy burden on the returned exiles and lord it over them. Instead, he said, "Out of reverence for God, I did not act like that. Instead, I devoted myself to the work on this wall" (Neh. 5:15–16 NIV). He sought nothing for himself, only the furtherance of the kingdom of God on the earth. He was loyal.

Loyal men do not tell tales. "A talebearer reveals secrets, / But he who is of a faithful spirit conceals a matter" (Prov. 11:13).

In nations' capitals around the world governments experience what are called "leaks," which become problems to those who govern and to those who are governed. These "leaks" are caused by people who tell things in public that they heard in secret. People who "leak," or murmur, are loyal not to their superior's agenda, but to their own.

Loyal church members do not gossip, find fault, or murmur against their pastor. Neither do they listen to rumors from known sources of such things.

Confidentiality is a virtue of the loyal, just as loyalty is a virtue of the faithful.

Pastors who hear things in private and repeat them publicly are not loyal and, therefore, not faithful.

A man came to me complaining he was getting passed over for

promotion. As I listened, I discovered that he was openly negative about the people he worked for, showed little loyalty, and then wondered why he failed to receive a promotion. He was fortunate he wasn't fired.

The other element of faithfulness is *submission*. Personal submission is willingly yielding, giving, or offering yourself to an authority. Conversely, sedition is revolting against authority to which one owes allegiance. Submission is God's answer to sedition. Sedition in the Church today is ripping apart congregations, tearing down families, and crushing friendships. To remain faithful today, a man must beware of the subtlety of sedition.

In the aftermath of the public display of ministerial misdeeds, where loss of respect occurred in both the secular and sacred populations, blasphemy broke out in the secular arena and sedition in the sacred.

Romans 2 says that when ministers preach against adultery and then engage in it, or lecture not to covet and then show greed for money, or forbid others to steal and then are found in thievery, it causes blasphemy among unbelievers. Nathan the prophet told King David that his adultery with Bathsheba caused blasphemy against the worthy name of Jehovah.

As loss of respect is the number one cause of divorce in marriages, so it is in the relationship between parishioner and pastor. When loss of respect for the ministry occurs through ministers' offenses or malfeasance, the authority in the church is shaken. Loss of respect often causes sedition. The Bible calls sedition a "work of the flesh." Galatians 5:19–21 lists sedition right up there with gross vices such as adultery, murder, witchcraft, and idolatry.

Sedition is an act of treason. It is the undermining of constituted authority with an attempt to overthrow it. In the American justice system, sedition can be punishable by death.

Responsible governments in nations around the world have been destroyed by sedition. Great tragedies, untold human suffering, and financial debacles are the results of sedition in civic affairs. "Office coups," where chief executive officers are ousted and the seditious in spirit take over, almost always spell the decline or ruin of the company.

Many Christians have grown up understanding the evils of drunkenness, reveling, fornication, and heresy, but little is understood of sedition, which the Bible lists with these damnable sins. Good citizens, family and church members, reject the thought of treason, yet engage in it unknowingly. Sedition is natural to the human heart, a product of the soul of man in its rebellious nature.

These are not the works of the devil as some suppose, but the works of human nature apart from the control of the Holy Spirit. You can't overcome adultery by "casting out the devil" when adultery is a work of the flesh. Adultery is overcome by "mortifying the members of the flesh" (Col. 3:5 KJV), dying to lustful desires, rendering as dead the old self for which Christ died to resurrect as a "new creation" (Eph. 2:1–5).

Sedition also must be dealt with ruthlessly to get it out of the life. But first we must recognize it. For example, children are the number one cause of arguments between parents which, once started, can evolve into callousness that can eventually lead to divorce. A seditious act can be as simple as one parent's not enforcing the same discipline on the children.

An illustration of it occurred the other day when Bill was talking about his three-year-old daughter, whom he described as "the cutest and most adorable child ever born." When her mother refused her request for a piece of candy she crawled up into Bill's lap and asked for it with a "cutesy" smile, a kiss, and a big hug. Bill gave it to her. What he did not realize was that he was acting seditiously against his wife, undermining and overthrowing her authority in the mind of their daughter. Later in life, when his selfish, manipulative daughter demands her own way, he will have forgotten that he sowed those first seeds in his daughter's life himself. What a large fire a little kindling can start. What seems so innocuous can become disastrous.

When Tom gave his son permission to have the car for an evening to take his girlfriend on a date, the son was told to have the car back home by 10:30 P.M. When he finally came home at 2:30 A.M., Tom was furious, took the keys from his son, and said, "You're grounded for thirty days. Don't ask for the car!"

The following week when the son wanted the car, he appealed to his mother who said yes. Knowing what her husband had said, but acting in sympathy with the son, she was seditiously eroding her husband's stance. She was teaching the son to disrespect his father's word. She thought she was being kind, not realizing that she was actually committing domestic treason.

Don't think me harsh. These treasonous little occurrences produce animosity, antagonism, and hardness of heart that lead so often to anarchy among the children and divorce in the parents. Unrecognized as rebellion, the damage is incalculable.

"Church splits" are more often than not caused by the underlying work of seditious spirited people trying to overthrow the pastor.

An attitude of submission to one another will stop the spread of sedition. No wonder the Bible says to "submit to God" (James 4:7) and "[submit] to one another in the fear of God" (Eph. 5:21).

Even the withholding of tithes, hoping to cause financial distress that will cause the pastor to resign, is an act of sedition.

Submission is the solution to sedition.

Sedition is one of many forms of rebellion. In His parable of the prodigal son, Jesus gives a pattern of societal downfall and restoration: rebellion, ruin, repentance, reconciliation, restoration. The prodigal's rebellion was not outright anarchy, but a desire for independence from the father's authority (Luke 15:11–32). Sin in its basic form is a denial of God's right of possession. Men who desire independence from God the Father and want to live their lives apart from His will are, in fact, rebels against God, who created them.

People came to Ezekiel in his day to hear what he had to say, but then they paid no attention to it (Ezek. 33:30–33). Their rebellion expressed itself in indifference. Jeremiah, before he prophesied, elicited a promise from those listening that they would submit to whatever they heard as a word from the Lord. But when they heard the word that was counter to their desires, they rejected it (Jer. 38:15); their rebellion was in the rejection of God's Word.

Absalom rebelled against his father King David. He sat by the entrance to the city, counseling, consoling, and conferring with the people, winning their confidence, while whispering to them that if he were king he would be different from his father. In this way he stole the hearts of the people, caused them to participate in his seditious uprising, betrayed his father's trust, subverted the throne, and wreaked havoc on the country. God would not tolerate Absalom's sedition, and Absalom met an ignoble death (2 Sam. 15:1–6, 18:9–15).

At a ministers' meeting in New York, I talked about the sin of sedition, its horrible nature and dire consequences. When the meeting ended a man walked up, put his arms around me, and began to cry as he whispered, "I didn't know."

When he composed himself, he confided, "About ten months ago a brother from a church I used to attend called me and asked if I would work with him in a new church he was starting.

"He had been an associate pastor when I knew him, and we were friends. So I told him I'd come and help. About four months ago I noticed a change in my daughters, and three months ago I sensed a rebellious attitude. They had never been like that before, and I couldn't figure out what had happened.

"Then a few weeks ago my wife began to talk about divorce. Here I was trying to do everything I knew to be a good husband, father, church member, and my whole life was coming apart. Today, when I heard you talk about sedition, it hit me. The pastor I came to help had started his congregation with a 'split' from the church where he had been an associate. I didn't think much about it because it happens all the time. But right now I realize that he had a seditious spirit when he left. When I put my family in his congregation they embraced his spirit, and his attitude got into the heart of my family."

After I shared that man's story, another wrote this: "I write you because for four long years I have been searching for an answer. In 1987 I closed the doors of my church because my wife and family could not stand it any longer. After we left we discovered I had taken over a group of people that had split from another church together with the assistant pastor.

"When I accepted that pastorate, troubles at home broke out. My daughters split up with their husbands, my oldest son had problems with his wife. My life hit an all-time low. I left the church and ministry feeling like a failure and wondering what had happened.

"Today when you told about the man in New York who suffered from a spirit of sedition in the pastor he joined, *I saw myself.* I had taken a rebellious people and, rather than my helping them, they almost ruined me.

"Today I repented, forgave them and the assistant who got me into that mess, prayed with my wife. . . . Now I can't wait to minister to the rest of my family. Thank you."

People can engage in sedition when they are not in submission to rightful authority.

If you have been the victim of sedition, engaged in it, infected by it, then in the name of God get it out of your life! In the parable of the

Prodigal you can see that repentance is the pivotal point between ruin and reconciliation. Repent! Pray!

When a faithful man has been unfaithful he is faithful to repent. Show yourself a faithful man.

Faithful in the little, faithful in another man's, constant, loyal, submissive—Christlike.

Chapter 11
Nothing but the Truth

There was a scuba diver off the coast of Florida who had invested in every bit of paraphernalia his sport offered. During a dive one day he saw a man swim by in just a bathing suit. Then he swam by again. The diver was amazed. Finally, when the man came around again, the diver took out his underwater slate and wrote, "I paid thousands of dollars to do this, and you're doing it in just a swim suit. How do you do it?" The swimmer read the slate, took the underwater pen, and wrote, "I'm drowning, dummy."

As old as that joke is, it still points to a moral: Things aren't always as they seem. Viewing from a limited perspective does not tell the whole story. All our understanding is practical, at best, and only God, who is completely omniscient, totally understands all that is in the world—and in people.

God is the Creator; men are discoverers. We discover gold, and laws such as gravity or aerodynamics, and truth. Truth is human-kind's greatest discovery in life. Just as men work to discover precious metal so we must labor to discover truth. Wisdom is found only when sought with the same tenacity, fierceness, and effort as seeking gold. Neither truth nor wisdom are found lying on the surface of life's strata.

We only discover Jesus as Truth when we remove the encrusted layers of our souls through the process of repentance and the exercise of faith. We must work to discover and embrace truth, regardless of the personal cost.

Jesus constantly worked to change the philosophies, mind-sets, attitudes, and thought patterns of His disciples. So much of what they knew and learned came from sources other than godly understanding of truth. Jesus, the Bible teaches, is Truth. As Truth it was His basic ministry to teach, represent, and reveal truth as it is in the very nature of God. Jesus indicted the religious Pharisees for embracing tradition at the expense of truth, and for rejecting truth when they heard it because it was contrary to their personal desires. Jesus praised those who understood truth as He revealed it, especially those truths related to His identity and mission.

Jesus Christ said, "I am the way, the truth, and the life" (John 14:6). Truth is the fulcrum for both the way and the life. The "way" is our direction in life, the "truth" is the moral and intellectual basis for life, the "life" is the result of our relationship to Jesus. The more we base our life on truth, the better will be our way and the greater will be our life.

Truth in its relational form is any element of knowledge that frees the mind and heart from error and lies. In its application it may be simple truth relating to a friend that clears a misunderstanding, an assumption wrongly deduced that is patently cleared by understanding, or even the basis for friendship.

The power of truth is liberating.

Jesus said, "You shall know the truth, and the truth shall make you free" (John 8:32). Satan is said to blind men's minds (2 Cor. 4:4), and thus enslave them, but when the truth is seen, they are freed from the power that held them.

VALUE OF TRUTH

Truth is one of life's most valuable commodities, if not the *most* valuable, yet we disregard it in society today. A national American magazine featured an article about the U.S. concerning lying, cheating, and stealing. ABC News spent an entire television hour tracing the decline of American morals and the same three characteristics marking national life, also entitled "Lying, Cheating, Stealing: Ethics in Modern America."[1] U.S. legislators pass "truth in advertising" laws because marketers cannot be trusted to be truthful, and even then law enforcement officers spend millions trying to enforce such statutes.

A new American report on ethics led to this incriminating headline: "Did We Rear a Bunch of 'Moral Mutants'?" The report's researcher and author foresees in our future "legions of young job applicants claiming degrees they don't have to get jobs they aren't qualified for. . . . a tooth-and-nail scramble for economic survival, reward and prestige that will trample proper conduct, honesty and altruism." Seventy-five percent of high-school students and 50 percent of college students admit to cheating. In business, 12 to 30 percent of job applications contain "deliberate inaccuracies." The report concluded, "This generation is the price we are paying for our own moral deterioration."[2]

Lest adults cluck their tongues at the young, they are targeted by another researcher who found "a tremendous craving among young people for honesty from adults."

There is so little reverence for truth that the entire world today suffers horribly from the lack. When Isaiah cried, "Truth is fallen in the street" (Isa. 59:14), his society had already begun to collapse.

Dictatorial governments practice "disinformation," lawyers "bend the truth," secretaries "falsify" reports, children tell "white lies," even preachers speak "evangelistically"—which is often nothing but a euphemism for exaggeration or lying.

Communism's foundation was a lie, propagated throughout the world. Even many intellectuals embraced it, saying it was the answer to democracy's ills. Now that we see communism's true nature with all its evils, poverty, and pain, the truth reveals the lie and is setting nations and people free.

Some greedy doctors bring reproach on medicine by pushing the limits of truth and doing surgeries needlessly just to collect the insurance. Their profession shakes because of it. This is a lamentable condition but one that seems to find a counterpart in many other professions.

Truth, individually and corporately, is the only viable absolute that is a foundation for societal stability. The human heart is deceitful and desperately wicked, without natural love for truth, which leaves a void where honesty, integrity, and other moral qualities should spring from.

When truth is discovered its reality brings change. To change the corporate community the individual must change. When change comes it elevates the level of life for both the community and the individual.

An automobile parts dealer admitted that he finally understood why he was losing his business. For years he had told every customer he could deliver their orders, whether he could or not. He was afraid to lose business, so he made promises he couldn't keep and suffered irreparable loss. People couldn't trust him, so they left him. He learned the value of truth. Built on a lie his business was failing, but converted to truth it began to succeed.

George is a man who suffered when he told the truth, but gained more than he ever lost. Just two weeks out of prison, he came to work for the Christian Men's Network and has been with us since. Now he tells his story all over the country. Four years ago when George came to know Christ, following a drug binge that caused him to cry out to God for help, his first thoughts were to do the right thing. Because he had warrants out for him in several states due to criminal activity, he immediately turned himself in to the authorities. He thought because he was doing the right thing and telling the truth, he would find leniency. It was a shock when he received a twenty-year sentence. He couldn't understand why for the first time when he acted honorably the authorities would treat him as they did. He thought God would have honored his honesty and caused them to let him go free.

God didn't intervene for two and a half years, then miraculously those same authorities granted George's release. Now, in retrospect, George can see where the years he served in a series of prisons became his "Bible school." He used that time to study the Bible, witness, minister, pray. Sometimes he was mocked for his faith and commitment, but it all worked together to make him into a strong Christian.

Through the experience he gained firsthand knowledge of prison systems, from the city to the national level. After leading 150 inmates to Christ, George left with a vision of a ministry to men and the knowledge of how to reach them with the gospel even when behind bars. Today, instead of a hardened, drug-addicted criminal, he and his wife spend their evenings ministering to inmates' families, weekends visiting prisons, and one day hope to have a full-time prison ministry. Now he thanks the Lord for the courage to stand for the truth, even though at first it landed him behind bars as a criminal. Truth was both his defense and offense.

CRISIS IN TRUTH MEANS A CRISIS IN TRUST

Trust is extended to the limit of truth and no more.
We trust what we believe to be true. When we believe nothing is

true, we trust nothing. Perception is not necessarily what is true. Perception can be deception.

The loss of truth spawned today's lack of trust. People who trust less are often alienated from those around them. One columnist purports that we no longer "watch out" for the company we work for and trust it to "watch out" for us.[3] Instead, everyone looks out for number one: self. Stand-up comedienne Lily Tomlin joked sadly, "We're all in this alone."

Trust is restored when truth is restored as the basis of individual character and the relationships of life.

Real men are trusted because they are lovers of truth—the whole truth. A half-truth is a whole lie. Truth mingled with lies and half-truths is no longer truth. Only truth is truth! To trust beyond the truth is to trust in a lie.

There was an ancient principle God handed down to the Israelites: Don't sow with "mixed seed" (Lev. 19:19). God forbade them to mix animals under yoke, linen with wool, their children with neighboring nations. "Keep yourself pure" became the New Testament injunction (1 Tim. 5:22). We cannot base our lives on God's Word mixed with lies from a decadent society. Those who teach psychological principles that are straight from the wisdom of God as revealed in His Word are often of great help to humanity. Those who mix humanistic psychology with the truths of God's Word do humanity a disservice. Corrupting the Cross by minimizing Christ's sacrifice brings confusion.

Deceitfulness is one of the characteristics of sin.

- Unbelief is the basis of sin.
- Pride is the strength of sin.
- Deceitfulness is the nature of sin.

No lie will ever serve the purposes of God. Nothing built on a lie will stand. Men cannot allow themselves to become so cynical that they no longer recognize truth and assume everyone is telling a lie. Knowledge of the Bible, and the guidance of the Holy Spirit, is essential to know what is truth and what is not. Lying is an evil work, and bears the mark of the author, Satan, who is the father of all lies (John 8:44). All lies lead to death; liars are no better off.

Of any people who should be trustworthy in community life, it is those who preach the gospel. Too often, though, this is not so. And sometimes this works to the detriment of those who are honest.

At one time our ministry had a radio broadcast called "Maximized Manhood." There came a time when it was financially inadvisable to continue, and we told our listeners for several weeks that we would have to go off the air due to lack of support. Only after we were no longer broadcasting were we deluged with letters. Many thought our very real plea was a ploy to elicit funds and said apologetically, "We didn't believe you." We told the truth, but our listeners didn't believe us. What a sad commentary!

RESPONDING TO TRUTH

Job said, "Just as my mouth can taste good food, so my mind tastes truth when I hear it" (Job 12:11 LB). Developing a taste for truth creates a love for it.

Look at the difference in the ways King David and King Saul in the Bible responded to truth. Their responses displayed their attitudes toward truth and God. Their attitudes and subsequent actions determined their destinies.

David committed adultery with Bathsheba, then ordered her husband Uriah killed (2 Sam. 11–12). The murder was a cover-up for his transgression of God's commandment and an attempt to justify his relationship with her. Months passed without David voluntarily repenting. God finally sent the prophet Nathan to confront David.

Nathan wisely told David about an unjust wealthy man who was trying to take a little lamb from a helpless poor person. Nathan's story incensed David and he wanted to know who could do such a thing. Nathan looked David eyeball to eyeball and thundered, "Thou art the man!" Stricken with guilt before God, ashamed before man, David fell on his face in deep repentance. As a lover of truth, when David heard it, he immediately went before God in sackcloth and ashes to seek God's forgiveness (2 Sam. 12; Ps. 51).

At an earlier time, a prophet reproved King Saul for a different transgression. He and the prophet Samuel agreed to meet at a certain place for Samuel to offer a sacrifice to God for the people. Saul arrived first and grew impatient. Tired of waiting for Samuel, he "forced himself" and offered the sacrifice, something he knew was strictly forbidden by God. When Samuel confronted him for disobeying God's Word, Saul blamed the people for his sin. Faced with the truth, Saul sought to transfer blame and guilt to others, rather than accept the truth and admit his error. As a result, God removed Saul from the throne and took away his kingdom (1 Sam. 13:5–14).

The difference between David and Saul was in their love of the truth. Saul did not love truth and rejected it when he heard it. David loved truth and repented when he heard it. David is referred to as a man after God's heart, not because he repented but because he loved truth (1 Sam. 13:14). Saul lost his kingdom and died prematurely. David retained his kingdom and became part of the lineage of the King of kings, Jesus, whose kingdom is eternal. The result of David's sin brought suffering to David and his kingdom, but he remained king until he died in his old age.

Real men are not perfect. We strive for the ideal, but live the real. When we sin and face the truth, repentance is the way to rightness before God. When a man is willing to do right after being wrong—humble, contrite, repentant—God in His mercy forgives, reconciles, and restores him to a right relationship with God.

To hide the sin and ignore the truth is to bring God's Word to reality: "There is nothing concealed that will not be disclosed, or hidden that will not be made known" (Luke 12:2 NIV). "Be sure your sin will find you out" (Num. 32:23).

In recent days respect for a man I've known for many years has reached new dimensions of admiration, appreciation, and affection. I'll call him Jerry. When we met he was in the process of recovering from public disclosure of his private infidelities and dismissal from his pulpit. As he went through the throes of his agonies, attempting to maintain his marriage, seeking to reconcile his children, and doing it an attitude of submission to discipline, I could not help but admire his honesty and integrity.

His open admission of wrong, sincere desire to make restitution, earnest employment of Bible study, eventually brought him back to the pulpit he had thought was lost. The highest form of restoration for a man who has sinned is to be restored to the place he was before.

A LACK OF TRUTH LEADS TO LACK OF RESPECT

Dr. James Dobson of "Focus on the Family" attributes loss of respect as the underlying cause of most troubled marriages in America today.[4] When a woman can no longer respect a man because she cannot trust his word, she no longer wants to bear his name. When a man no longer respects a woman because he cannot trust her, he no longer wants her to share his life.

Years ago my wife worked at a large laboratory to help us make ends meet on my pastoral salary. We were getting along well, but the emotional distance between us began to grow. Not intense arguments, but petty little picky things, unsettling and unnerving. Like barbs under the skin, they were poison to our attitude.

One Monday morning I was sitting in the church office with my staff seated around me. Nancy was on her way to work. The staff and I were going over yesterday's blessings during Sunday's service and activities, talking about tomorrow's plans, and discussing what we could do to further the growth of the ministry.

At a moment of convivial laughter, the door opened and Nancy looked in. She saw me there with the staff in a very intimate conversation—to which she was not privy—and quickly closed the door. Slowly realizing what it must have meant to her, I jumped up and ran to intercept her, but she was in the car and gone.

That evening when she came home I tried to mollify her by telling her what was happening. She would have none of it. I had been basking in the glory of "my ministry," accepting the accolades of "my staff," getting my strokes of appreciation and affection—and she had no part of it. Our worlds were getting further apart.

That episode made me realize I had great respect for what I was doing, and little for what she was doing for the family. It started long periods of intense thought and prayer on the status of my marriage, ministry, and family. Thinking the ministry and marriage could be separated, and both be successful, I had believed a lie. As a result, I had become more intimate with my church staff than I was with my own wife and family. Though I had the respect of the congregation, I had lost Nancy's through neglect.

I also had to face the truth that I had encouraged Nancy to augment our income instead of going before the church to ask for a raise. Cowardice on my part, courage on hers, and now I was having to face my character defects and masculine inadequacies.

Jesus told us to go and make things right with others before we could come and offer our gifts upon the altar (Matt. 5:23–24). It was my responsibility to make right what I had made wrong.

To this day I wince as I think about those days. That is why I write as I do, to encourage other men to do right so they won't have to "reinvent the wheel."

Wife and family come before business, ministry, or career. God comes before wife and family. I had it inverted and had to be converted. Conversion is a constant, not only instant, process. Our freedom from wrong believing is dependent upon our discipline to receive truth. Only truth makes us free (John 8:32).

Once I accepted the truth, accepted responsibility for my actions, asked forgiveness of my wife and family, things began to change dramatically. Nancy and I agreed on a specific date when she would stop work and God honored the date by blessing our income. We then took a family vacation and began to live again as God intended—and the ministry never suffered one iota for the time I spent with my family!

TRUTH CARRIES A PRICE TAG

Truth is not cheap. Truth always costs. A man has to die to himself to accept the truth—and find new life through the dying. Calvary was the price God paid to give us Truth. As Christ died to make it possible to receive truth, we have to die—to self—to receive it. "Buy the truth, and do not sell it," the Bible says (Prov. 23:23).

Hold onto truth, not as your possession, but as your Savior and Master and Defender. Truth is your shield and strength. It is part of the "armor of God" to help us combat the "father of lies." Only truth can defeat a lie. It is our defense and offense in all our battles.

Truth is its own defense, and it is eternal. Men tried to kill Truth by crucifixion, but Truth rose again the third day, and *Truth lives!*

We live to the degree we abide in the Spirit of Truth.

Those who desire to become real men love truth.

Chapter 12
Love or Lust

You probably saw, as I did, at least some of the United States Senate Judiciary Committee's televised hearings on the nomination of Judge Clarence Thomas to the United States Supreme Court. The nomination proceedings investigated a sexual harassment charge, interrogating the judge and a woman accuser. They received national and worldwide television and radio exposure. Anita Hill charged Judge Thomas with making obscene, lascivious remarks to her and intimating his desire to have sex with her. He categorically denied any such remarks or suggestions. Although he was finally confirmed to sit on the highest judicial court in the land, the vote that put him there almost barred him because of Anita Hill's charges.

Newspapers that same week also reported the tragic story of a minister apprehended by police in the company of a prostitute. Pornographers recently have filed suit against those who are opposed to their publications. Pro-abortionists, advocating a liberal attitude toward sexual promiscuity, flail verbally and physically at pro-life advocates who are opposed to immorality. Dictators throughout the world use people for personal advantage without thought to the carnage or conflict created. The "decade of greed" in America has produced a recession, bankruptcies, banking crises, and a crippled government.

Serial killers (both homosexual and heterosexual), rapists, child molesters grab the front pages and headlines of our newspapers daily.

At the root of all this is a thing called—lust!

Wherever you look in the world you cannot help but see the decadence, devastation, and debacles the nature of lust has produced in human life. Yet, to talk of lust's nature and consequences in open terms is often considered "improper" by those called Christians.

Christianity is based on confession, not suppression. On the other hand, some people accuse Christians of talking too much about it.

Both extremes are absurd. All of us, whether we admit it or not, have to deal with lust every day. It may be something we see in ourselves or in the lives of others or society. But we know lust is active in our world.

Jesus knew lust's source, nature, causes, consequences, and suffered from those who were controlled and motivated by lust. He knew it far better than Freud, who equated lust and love. Freud desired to rid society of the Christian ethic of celibacy and morality and sought to excuse men from guilt caused by "religion." God's Word and Jesus Himself have the final word on love and lust.

LUST IS PERVERTED LOVE

In unveiling the love of God, Jesus taught love's principle with, "God so loved the world that He gave His only begotten Son, that whoever believes in Him should not perish but have everlasting life" (John 3:16).

The definition of *love* from what Christ said is this: Love is the desire to benefit others even at the expense of self because love desires to give. The moral opposite of love, though, is lust. So lust is the desire to benefit self at the expense of others because lust desires to get.

Any moral person who has ever been tempted by lust knows the power of that temptation, the battle that rages in the mind and heart to do or have something that would bring immediate pleasure, but negative long-term consequences.

The temptation to sin never comes parading the consequences of sin, but rather heralding the promises of the moment's pleasure. The great deception and seduction of sin is possible because temptation only shows immediate gratification. Blinded by the elation and ecstasy of the moment, everything else is erased from the mind. Only after realizing the moment's folly, and the price it will extract, does the awful reality of the consequences begin to set in.

The Bible says there is pleasure in sin (Heb. 11:25). Drunkenness, adultery, incest, drug abuse, embezzlement, rape, lying, stealing can bring pleasure, but such illicit delight lasts for a season. When the season is over, their pleasure turns to heartache and hardship.

Lustful desires in the lives of men who want to do right can be tormenting. Torn between right and wrong, pressured by conflicting passions, suffering in spirit, troubled in mind, confused in emotions, struggling to be free, the torment can be terrible. So terrible, in fact, that the thought of giving in and enjoying the momentary thrill can even seem too attractive to pass up.

Temptation can be tormenting, but remember: *The torment of the temptation to sin is nothing to compare with the torment of the consequences of sin.*

Remorse and regret cannot compensate for sin. Many times my daughter, Lois, a prosecuting attorney, has told me of the tears, suffering, and pain of people tried for manslaughter caused by driving drunk. Many times I have counseled the adulterer who wishes to turn back the clock and regain the respect, trust, and love of his family lost by the practice of indulging sinful pleasure. Although they wish they could do it over, no amount of anguish or apology can change what happened.

Though sins can be forgiven immediately—the consequences can last a lifetime.

The first chapter of Romans describes the condition of men "burning" in their lusts. That "burning" is an emotional desire so strong it overcomes all logic and reason, consumes sanity by fires of passion, and causes seemingly uncontrollable actions.

When a man allows this burning to consume him, the consequent perversion allows him to justify any action, thought, or desire. He tries to rationalize away guilt and condemnation, deny their reality, even blame others for their existence. The Sodomites of biblical days fell prey to this chain of consequences. Through the deceitfulness of their sin they eventually became conscienceless, engaging in any form of iniquity and applauding without guilt those who invented new forms of evil (Gen. 19:4–5). They considered it to be an exercise of their free will, insisting on their individual rights at the expense of the corporate good.

The new "illness" of sexual addiction, amply written about in periodicals and books, is this uncontrolled lust seen in ancient days. What has brought it to public attention today are the incredible numbers of people whose sexual appetites interfere with the rest of their lives. The literature on the subject lists warning signs of sexual addiction: sexual thoughts that interfere with work and family; spending more money than is available to feed sexual desires; curtailing important relationships because of uncontrollable sexual behaviors; using sex as an escape; and risking AIDS or other diseases just to have sexual activity.[1]

The pleasures of sin exist. We cannot deny them. But we also dare not deny what follows in their wake: a voracious appetite, inflamed with eroticism, demanding more indulgence more often until a degenerative spiral captures the soul and drags us on a never-ceasing descent into deeper patterns of immorality and illicit behavior.

Lust goes beyond the sexual. Lust can show itself in a variety of forms: covetousness, gluttony, drunkenness, power hunger, or unbridled ambition, to name a few. But lust in any form knows no peace. Peace can only come through the "Prince of Peace," the Lord Jesus Christ, through the power of His Spirit.

TEMPTATIONS OF LUST

When we experience temptation and overcome it, we actually torment the tempter. Just as there is torment for the godly in the presence of the unclean and lustful, there is also torment for uncleanness and lust in the presence of the godly. Jesus confronted an unclean spirit in the synagogue one day. The spirit cried out saying, "Let us alone! What have we to do with You, Jesus of Nazareth? Did You come to destroy us?" (Luke 4:34). A legion of demons in another man cried out, "Have You come here to torment us before the time?" (Matt. 8:29).

The unclean are discomfited in the company of the clean, and the clean are uncomfortable in the presence of the unclean. Just as there is a vast chasm between heaven and hell, so is there a vast disparity between the righteous and unrighteous. "An unjust man is an abomination to the righteous, / And he who is upright in the way is an abomination to the wicked" (Prov. 29:27).

Jesus overcame all temptations. Jesus faced and overcame what the first Adam succumbed to, and made it possible for all men to overcome temptation through the power of His Spirit indwelling them. Jesus forever changed the nature of temptation from an occasion of defeat to an opportunity for victory.

When Jesus was tempted on the mountain, He met the tempter (Satan) and his temptations in three basic forms. Jesus never dealt with peripheral issues, but with basic issues of life and death. By dealing with temptations at their basic level, He showed His overcoming power over all temptations. Jesus was tempted to turn stone to bread because He was hungry, to bow to Satan in order to gain the kingdoms of the world, and to throw Himself off the pinnacle of the Temple to prove His power.

Two of these three temptations stem from lust. The Bible says, "All that is the world—the lust of the flesh, the lust of the eyes, and the pride of life—is not of the Father but is of the world" (1 John 2:16). Jesus fought these same temptations.

An Old Testament parallel is found in the temptation of Eve in Eden, which resulted in the "Fall of Man." Eve saw that the tree was "good for food, that it was pleasant to the eyes, and a tree desirable to make one wise" (Gen. 3:6). She was tempted by the three basic temptations all at once. She took the fruit, shared it with Adam, and humanity has lived with the consequences of their sin ever since.

LUST OF THE FLESH

"It's not what you know, but who you know" is an old adage predicated on the truth of the gospel: You don't get to heaven based on what you know, but Who you know. Knowing about church, the Bible, and Jesus is not the same as knowing God. But when we come to know God and place faith in Him through Jesus, we receive eternal life (John 17:3).

People, however, often pervert this principle through selfishness. They use people for personal advantage. Things are *loved* and people *used* to acquire fame, fortune, power, or pleasure.

In sexual matters and relationships, lust causes men to see women as sex objects. This attitude reduces men to predators and women to prey. It creates abnormal thought patterns, causes mental confusion, and perverts the normal reasoning process by desensitizing the conscience.

Pornography, which has been a plague in the lives of so many men, is a financially viable industry because it panders to the basest emotions. And many men obviously enjoy the titillation.

A total of 27,560,000 men subscribe to pornographic magazines, compared to 13,034,000 who subscribe to *Sports Illustrated*. Even in nonpornographic magazines, and especially in advertising, women are treated as sex objects more often than as human beings, much less joint-heirs of God's blessing.

"The lamp of the body is the eye. Therefore, when your eye is good, your whole body also is full of light," Jesus taught in his Sermon on the Mount (Matt. 6:22; Luke 11:34). A pure eye lets sunshine into your soul. A lustful eye shuts out light and plunges the soul into darkness. "To the pure all things are pure, but to those who are defiled and unbelieving nothing is pure" (Titus 1:15). Men corrupted and contaminated by lust see nothing pure in others, either in motive or deed. They ascribe to others a perspective colored by their polluted minds.

Ted Bundy, before his execution, attributed the atrocities of his multiple murders to pornography. A pornographer's fantasy life, incapable of existing in normal behavior, produces an unrealistic approach to life. For Bundy it resulted finally in illusions of the mind that never found self-gratification even in murder.[2]

A minister in Dallas pleaded guilty to five counts of aggravated sexual assault and received ten concurrent life terms in prison. He said that viewing pornographic films and magazines contributed to his behavior; that he started watching pornographic films with the football team in college and never stopped; and that he watched them just before committing his rapes.[3]

The Department of Justice reported that during a thirty-year period, from 1954 to 1984, there were 6,004 images of children portrayed in America's three best-selling sexually explicit magazines. Twenty-nine percent of the images depicted children nude and twenty percent related to genital activity. "Almost all" depictions of child sexual abuse portrayed the child as unharmed or benefited by the activity.[4]

A "happily married father of three" watched a "peep show" of a rape three times from beginning to end. Believing that in real life a little girl would enjoy it like in the movie, he did the same thing to a nine year old. Only "it didn't go that way," he said afterward. "I just wanted to die, crawl up in a hole and die, but it didn't stop there. I still wanted to see more movies."[5] His lusts were virtually insatiable, devastating innocent little girls while leading him to ruin.

The world before the flood degenerated until "the LORD saw that the wickedness of man was great in the earth, and that every intent of the thoughts of his heart was only evil continually" (Gen. 6:5). God's judgment on such a wicked and perverse generation was swift and sure. A flood wiped them out. Destruction also came upon Sodom. Fire rained from heaven and obliterated them without leaving so much as a trace of that society (Gen. 19:24–29). So it could be with our present world unless men turn to God and righteousness.

LUST OF THE EYES

This form of lust is basic covetousness. Covetousness is idolatry because it is basically the worship of self. The counterfeit trinity is "me, myself, and I." Self-pleasing is the pleasure principle upon which natural life rests. Pleasing God is the pleasure principle upon which godly life rests.

Lust's covetousness can cripple an entire society. It was the spirit of the 1980s in America. Sin was consummated on the highest levels of society from the lust that was conceived on the lowest levels of society in the rebelliousness of the 1960s. It found its voice in characters such as "Gordon Gekko" from the film *Wall Street,* who said, "Greed is good." Junk bonds, leveraged buy-outs, "greenmail," savings and loan fraud, bribes, all stemmed directly from lustful men who cared little or nothing of what their actions would do to the financial burden of the common citizen.

A nation's citizens pay a high penalty for years for the lusts of men who achieve a modicum of power in government or economics, men unbalanced in their avariciousness and consumed with their personal gain at the expense of others.

All dictators are lustful people. Ceausescu in Romania wasted extravagantly on his family while keeping the citizenry in nineteenth-century poverty and crusading to eliminate every vestige of Christ from his country. How ironic that a man so filled with an anti-Christ attitude would be assassinated on Christmas Day.

However, even his viciousness against Christ competes with some in the "Christian nation" called America. Some claim that Christianity is a threat to society because it does not hold to an "enlightened view" on sex education. This view includes what the U.S. Surgeon General urged: that sex education "must include information on heterosexual and homosexual relationships."[6] The philosophy is that Christianity needs to be excised from the national conscience.

RIGHTEOUSNESS IS GOOD

What is "pleasant to the eyes" is not always good.

When Eve saw what was "pleasant to the eyes," she denied God's command. She chose what she judged to be good, only to discover it was evil. In God's economy only what is righteous is good. If it is not righteous, it is unrighteous and, therefore, evil, no matter how we label it or pretend or reason otherwise.

A Jewish doctor wrote a sensitive article, "Why I Quit Doing Abortions." He told how he started performing abortions out of a compassionate desire to help women in turmoil. Soon he began seriously doubting himself, hated going to work, and his religious practices no longer gave him a sense of well-being. One day a married couple who sought an abortion decided to go ahead and have the baby when the doctor couldn't perform the abortion due to a medical technicality. Playing with this couple's child years later at a tennis club where they were all members struck the doctor's heart with the final blow. Had it not been for a technicality, he would have killed little Jeffrey as an infant, dismembering him "limb by limb."[7] Misguided compassion can kill. Only God can tell us what is truly "good."

The fear of the Lord is the restraint from doing evil. To remove the restraints, society now advocates sanctions against Christianity, virtually trying to dismiss God from our presence. To remove moral barriers in order to rid society of guilt is a form of civil suicide.

Planned Parenthood is a national organization founded by an admitted amoral social revolutionary devoted to the overthrow of moral restraint in America. In his book *Grand Illusions,* George Grant tells what Margaret Sanger, founder of Planned Parenthood, wrote in her first newspaper, *The Woman Rebel:*

> Birth control appeals to the advanced radical because it is calculated to undermine the authority of the Christian Churches. I look forward to seeing humanity free someday of the tyranny of Christianity no less than capitalism.

The organization she founded is still trying to break down moral barriers built by godly principles.[8]

LOVE, THE ANSWER TO LUST

The answer to lust is love. Lust is degenerative, love is regenerative.

When Jesus rebuked the hardened-of-heart religious practitioners of His day, He told them, "Ye are of your father the devil, and the lusts of your father ye will do" (John 8:44 KJV). Satan is the progenitor of lust. It began when he first lusted after God's throne, and he has never stopped. He still desires to be worshiped, and that motive is the cause for so many cults, false religions, and perverted philosophies in human society.

Men accused Jesus of having a devil and being unfair in His denunciation of them. He answered them, "I do not have a demon; but I honor My Father, and you dishonor Me" (John 8:49).

Lustful men dishonored the Lord by their accusations against Him, cried for His crucifixion because His holiness was a personal rebuke to their way of life, and so to rid themselves of guilt they decided to rid themselves of God.

Men carried away by lust are vicious, malicious, and murderous in their hatred of God. According to the Bible, they are heartless, faithless, and merciless in their pursuit of personal pleasure at the expense of what is good or righteous (Rom. 1:26–32).

Lust is insatiable; love is easily satisfied. A man who loves his wife finds her easily satisfying, while a man who lusts for his wife never finds satisfaction from her despite how hard she tries. No matter how she cares for him, submits her body to him, cleans the house, takes care of the children, pays the bills, works at a job, she will never quench his lustful thirst. Why? Because lust is self-centered, while love is other-centered. Lust appeals to our greed, while love appeals to grace. Greed can never be satisfied; it always wants more. Grace finds satisfaction in the restoration and happiness of others. Once that is achieved, even if it comes in stages, grace finds satisfaction. Blessed is the wife who is lavished with grace rather than lashed by lust.

OVERCOMING LUST THROUGH THE HOLY SPIRIT

Lust comes easier than love. Because we are fallen creatures, our natural propensity is to satisfy ourselves rather than reach out to others. Even when we are born again, the lusts of the old nature war against the members of the body, wanting them to do what they formerly enjoyed. But Scripture enjoins men to "walk in the Spirit, and you shall not fulfill the lust of the flesh" (Gal. 5:16). To "put off, concerning your former conduct, the old man which grows corrupt according to the deceitful lusts, and be renewed in the spirit of your mind" (Eph. 4:22–23). Renewing the mind means putting away lustful thoughts and conscientiously engaging in righteous thinking. The renewing process is to fill the mind with the Word and pray for the Holy Spirit's work of purging our lustful desires.

God charges real men today who have the Spirit of Christ to walk in the Spirit and not in the flesh, so they can be "more than conquerors," overcoming temptation and sin (Rom. 8:37). James wrote, "count it all joy when you fall into various trials" (James 1:2). When we are confronted by temptations and defeat them by not yielding, the work of Christ in us is perfected, which brings glory to God.

Job fought a battle with lust and came to an understanding of the only way to rise above it. "I have made a covenant with my eyes; / Why then should I look upon a young woman?" he wrote (Job 31:1). A covenant is a powerful tool in the mind and heart of men. When Job made that covenant with God it became a tool that helped keep him free from lust and maintain his integrity before God.

Consider Titus 2:11–12 (NIV):

> For the grace of God that brings salvation has appeared to all men. It teaches us to say "No" to ungodliness and worldly passions, and to live self-controlled, upright and godly lives in this present age.

If this were impossible, God would be in error to command it.

The pleasure of knowing you are a real man and ready to stand before God the Father is greater than any moment's pleasure this earthly world can give you.

Part 5

Real Accomplishments

■ ■ ■

Chapter 13

Royal Pursuits

It is Indian summer in Southern California. Warm breezes whisper through my window. I hear the neighbor's children laughing as they walk home from school. Someone is mowing a lawn, releasing the sweet, verdant fragrance into the air. My visiting daughter received flowers from her husband, and they sit between me and the window, their scent mixed with every breeze. Serenity in the home, peace in the neighborhood, affectionate closeness in the family make the day like paradise. A day like this makes you long for more. I often joke that where I live is the site of the New Jerusalem. A day like this makes it easy to think about heaven.

Heaven is part of the kingdom of God. The most heavenly part of living is really not the weather or our circumstances, but the degree to which we bring heaven to earth in our day-to-day living.

There are two moral or spiritual kingdoms in the world. First is the kingdom of God, which embraces all over which God rules and reigns, and the other exists as a result of Satan's anarchy against God. The kingdom of Satan is antagonistic and antithetic to the kingdom of God. It has ever been, and still is, Satan's purpose to take the place of God. Sedition began in heaven when Satan, then called Lucifer, no longer wanted to lead worship but to be worshiped. Lifted up with pride, he led a seditious assault on God and was expelled from heaven, wherein God created a place called hell for all those in rebellion against God.

Hell was originally created for Satan and the angels who fell with him, but when Satan usurped the place of God in man's life in Eden, it was enlarged to receive all who follow his pernicious pattern. Since the first man Adam lost his place with God, it behooved God to send another Adam to redeem human beings and restore them to the place God originally intended them to be—part of His family forever.

There are some things we all must learn and understand concerning the two kingdoms and our place in either of them. Every man lives in one of the two kingdoms. We are not born into the kingdom of God by natural birth, but when born of God's Spirit we both enter into His Kingdom and are able to "see" the kingdom of God (John 3:3).

When something is explained to another, and the other says, "Oh, I see now," he means that he understands what was said. In that sense seeing and understanding carry the same connotation. Here are some things we see, or understand, of the kingdom of God.

In the kingdom of God everything is positive, while in the kingdom of Satan everything is negative. Between the two there is constant tension.

God originally created human beings in the positive state of holiness and enjoyed fellowship with Adam and Eve, but when sin entered the very nature of man was changed from positive to negative and the fellowship was broken.

To restore man to the positive and enjoy fellowship with his Creator once more, God sent Christ into the world to reconcile men to Himself. When a man is translated into the kingdom of God from out of darkness through repentance and faith, he regains fellowship with God and enters into a positive relationship with Him.

The characteristics of the Kingdom emanate from the King, so all the characteristics in the kingdom of God are positive, and in the other kingdom are negative. Light vs. darkness. Truth vs. lies. Love vs. lust. Righteousness vs. sin. As each facet of the nature of God is revealed by the characteristics in His kingdom they are also seen in the negative in the opposite kingdom.

God is the Creator; Satan is the counterfeiter. Satan counterfeits everything God creates. For example, the corner barroom is a counterfeit church where the bartender is the pastor; people go there to find fellowship, receive counsel, and are filled with spirits. That's a counterfeit church!

All principles originate in the kingdom of God. There are no principles in Satan's kingdom, for he adheres to none. Perversions of principles come from Satan's domain. For example, there is a principle that prayer produces intimacy. One of Satan's perversions is to promise intimacy through pornography rather than prayer. Pornography promises the benefits, physical closeness, and good feelings of intimacy, but ultimately results in distance, addiction, impotence, and alienation.

Virtue flows from God's kingdom, but the root of all sin is in the kingdom of Satan. Remember, all sin promises to please and serve but only intends to enslave and dominate.

God's kingdom is moral, Satan's immoral. This is the reason men have never found a solution to man's immorality by natural means.

"Seek first the kingdom of God and His righteousness, and all these things shall be added to you" (Matt. 6:33). Men naturally seek those things in life that seem important, not realizing if they seek first the kingdom of God, then those in the natural will follow.

MINISTRY AND MONEY

Money follows ministry.

When men seek money before ministry, they will not accomplish much.

Ministry and money are both means of support. Money has no morality; it is amoral, and its only morality or immorality is in the heart of the holder. We give money its morality by how we use it, or its immorality by how we abuse it.

To have money men must first minister.

If you are my grandson and want money, you mow a neighbor's lawn or wash his car. Money follows. If you are a career person, you go to work and do a good job. You receive a paycheck in return for your ministry. As I write in my dining room today, there is a plumber upstairs in the bathroom replacing corroded fixtures. If you've ever needed a plumber, you know that plumbers do not work free, yet I have paid him nothing so far. He is ministering to my house so that my money will follow.

We are prone to think that ministry is just standing in a pulpit preaching, but the truth is, everything we do in serving is ministry. Cleaning a toilet is ministry. Selling a car is ministry. When you wire a house, repair broken pipes, turn a lathe, write a letter, you are ministering. The Bible says, "And whatever you do, do it heartily, as to the Lord" (Col. 3:23). When that Scripture motivates us, everything we do, from running a jackhammer to changing a diaper, has significance beyond the merely temporal.

Whatever a man does, when he serves as "unto the Lord," the Lord compensates. Many people believe when they are financially destitute or needy that somehow someone somewhere will appear to take care of them. That is "magical thinking." Others believe they must have money with which to start a business, but that also is a fallacy. The Bible says if we do not work, we do not deserve to eat (2 Thess. 3:10). When you are out of work and need money, go out and minister, and money will follow. There are examples all around you of men who saw a need, ministered to that need, and ended up building a successful business. When you want to start something new, don't think you can't because you don't have huge capital reserves. Start where you are, not where you want to be. "For who has despised the day of small things?" (Zech. 4:10).

FAITH AND FACTS

Facts follow faith.

Faith determines what the facts will be. The bookkeeper substantiates with facts what the executive did by faith. The fact of the profit and loss statement is not possible until something is done by faith. It takes faith to launch a business, to try a new marketing strategy, to secure a contract for a big job. Faith precedes; facts follow.

PRAYER AND PRODUCTION

The physical reciprocal to prayer is production.

When a man brings his prayers to bear upon his production, he can expect greater results. But, if he thinks all he has to do is pray and forget about production, he fails. Jesus is concerned about production, not just prayer. He said, in effect, "If it doesn't produce, lop it off" (Luke 13:9, my own paraphrase).

When a man becomes so spiritual he ceases to be productive, he can become "so heavenly minded that he is no earthly good." He must reckon with both kingdoms constantly. Prayer in the morning preceding the day's work augurs well for the day.

Some years ago it was my privilege to be associated with a Christian broadcasting ministry. When it first started the people who were attracted to it were people with a heart for God, but very little expertise in the media, either technically or theoretically. They were spiritual, prayerful, good people, full of faith and eager to volunteer. But eventually, as the venture grew, the ministry needed to have skills and production, not just the ability to pray. The danger was that over a period of time, as they grew, they didn't exchange the prayerful for the productive. Balance was needed.

And—interestingly enough—when the "only prayerful" were replaced by those who were more balanced, the leader was criticized by those who were supposed to be such paragons of prayer.

When profits are needed, a roomful of volunteers is wonderful, but even those must produce. As a friend of mine said after recovering from thirty months on the verge of bankruptcy, "Money is not the most important thing in the world, but when you need money—it is the most important thing!"

Prayer precedes production, but production is the evidence of prayer. A praying man who produces is far more valuable than one who had either but not both of those qualities. "Praying producers" are always in demand.

SPIRITUAL AND PROFESSIONAL

Professionals who are prayerful and productive are indispensable! I understand how, out of zeal and an eagerness to please God, men can get wrapped up in what they believe is the religious or spiritual part of life to their own hurt. A friend of mine is in distress today because he would not stop witnessing on the job when his boss asked him to tone it down a little. His boss didn't violate his faith, or command him to stop, he just said not to take so much company time to witness. Loss of production caused loss of respect.

We want greater results, not lesser. In God's kingdom you are concerned about the spiritual—ministry, faith, prayer, and things that are eternal. At work you are concerned about making a living, building a reputation, seeing a good profit and loss statement. You can feel torn between the two until you have sought God in the spiritual, followed it with the professional, and found the balance between them. Balance is the key to life.

When trying to find your balance, establish your priorities first:

Seeking first the kingdom of God causes things of this life to follow. Money, facts, production, professional are all in the temporal realm, while ministry, faith, prayer, spirituality are all in the eternal.

Seeking first the eternal causes the temporal to follow.

Seeking first the temporal misses the eternal. The eternal is always more important than the temporal.

ORGANISMS AND ORGANIZATIONS

God creates organisms but the world creates organizations. Organisms do not deal with "political expediency," organizations do. Political expediency is the attempt to keep everything at peace through compromise. Committee members often seek to avoid personal responsibility for the outcome, to their own hurt.

Most organizations deal in political expediency and pluralities, work by committee, make decisions based on compromise, avoid accountability, and attempt to satisfy everyone. God's organisms, however, deal with the singular, operate through a visionary, make decisions based on principle, accept accountability, and attempt to please God. This is why God did not create the Church as a great organization, but as the Body of Christ, an organism. In that Body, God doesn't call a committee to lead a local church by compromise, but a visionary, to whom the Lord adds those needed to carry out the vision. God's provision is always ministry, men, and money. God gives the vision, adds men, and money follows.

Doing things by compromise or by committee at times is not wrong, except that it is so easy for everyone to try to satisfy everyone, and no one is pleased. God tells men to please Him, and He'll take care of everyone else (Prov. 16:7). The man who seeks to please God is most likely to have people pleased with him. The closer a man is to God the more a man of the people he becomes.

Company executives and church leaders are most successful when in agreement with themselves and their goals, than when they try to agree with employees and congregations. It's far easier for a thousand to agree with one than one to agree with a thousand.

TOUCH AND METHOD

Every place Jesus went, He touched people and healed them, although His method varied with the circumstances. The method always brought a reaction, but the touch brought the result. Perversion occurs through distortion when we teach the method and reward the reaction instead of teaching the touch and rewarding the result.

The method of the disciples was to evangelize in the marketplace. Today our message has not changed, but our method has. The contemporary marketplace is in media and communications, not just the open-air marketplace, so the gospel is literally going around the world on television and radio. The touch and results are the same; the method and reactions are different.

CONSTANT AND INSTANT

Jesus' touch was constant; His method was instant. In our present society where instant gratification has become a way of life, some churches have "McDonaldized" the gospel, creating "microwave Christians" who are frustrated when God doesn't instantly "fax" them an answer to prayer. God is not concerned with the instant. The Church is not a drive-through franchise dispensing cookie-cutter Christians. God is concerned about the constant, and that is why His Word says the anointing "abides" (1 John 2:27). Jesus said, "If you abide in Me, and My words abide in you, you will ask what you desire, and it shall be done for you" (John 15:7). He did not say, "If you experience me and I experience you. . . ."

The constant is the objective and the instant is the subjective. When struggling in any situation, God can bring objectivity into life through prayer and the reading of His Word, because Christ is the "Counselor." When dealing with business, your family, a broken relationship, God's perspective will always be your most objective—and correct.

By abiding in God, applying the constant, you will find yourself becoming "instant in season and out," ready at the right time with the right word, right proposal, right idea.

INTERNAL AND EXTERNAL

Man sees the outside, is concerned with talent, and focuses on works. God looks on the heart (1 Sam. 16:7), is concerned with character, and sees worth.

Remember, Abraham pitched his tents but built his altars (Gen. 13:4). Man creates a problem for himself when he begins to pitch his altars and build his tents. It is a difference in value. You can pitch personality, but you must build character.

In the church, God wants pillars who support the work, not posts who just pitch in. When the pressure comes, those who are "pillars" help stabilize the church; those who are "posts" collapse under the weight of responsibility.

Principles are constant but personalities are instant. One who has "pitched" his personality can change in a minute. One who has built his character on principle is steadfast. When the internal is godly, the external shows it.

In seeking God's kingdom, then, the priorities are: the constant, the touch, results, the internal, and character, while the instant, the method, reactions, the external, talent, and personality follow.

Look at the second part of that verse: "and all these things shall be added to you" (Matt. 6:33). This is where we get that piece of heaven into our lives.

SUCCESS AND FAILURE

Success and failure are common to man.

People have a natural fear of failure, based on the fear of death. We are preconditioned to failure because everything in the natural is subject to failure. Stars fall, earth quakes, seas rage, men lie, buildings fall, and the earth grows old. To escape failure men spend millions of dollars annually trying to discover a way.

There is one surefire way to overcome failure: Be successful.

God has a plan for success delineated in Joshua 1:7–8. This is a passage you can meditate on daily until it becomes real in your own heart. God's plan is just two steps. First we must be converted from the negative to the positive. From darkness to light, fear to faith, death to life. We must believe God is working for our highest good, that what He has promised He will perform. This occurs when we are translated from the kingdom of Satan to the kingdom of God.

And we must meditate on His Word and adhere to it. God's Word is the sole source of our faith, and the absolute rule of our conduct. God's promise assures us that meditating on the Word to become a doer of it will bring success (Josh. 1:8).

The outcome, God says, is that "you may prosper wherever you go" and "you shall deal wisely and have good success." Simply stated, but the challenge of a lifetime to enact.

Acquiring wisdom and achieving success is not for the faint-hearted or mediocre. Overcoming barriers in our lives is not always instantaneous but, by seeking God's kingdom first, change will begin.

Doug is a twenty-two year old whose life was transferred into the kingdom of God, but in stages. His father was a violent alcoholic who abused him physically, mentally, emotionally, and sexually. At thirteen, Doug discovered pornography and began to gratify himself with fantasies and masturbation. Throughout his teen years he repeatedly tried suicide and became a heavy drinker.

At nineteen, a woman he dated introduced him to Christ, but he continued in his worldly habits. Two years later Doug found himself back in church, and this time he was gloriously converted. The drinking stopped instantly. But the pornography, fantasy, and masturbation continued. Months of guilt, remorse, prayer, and relapse followed. Then one day someone showed him one of our videos, *The Glory of Virginity,* and after earnestly and seriously digesting the truth of God's Word his life changed dramatically. Successfully overcoming his addictions gave him worth, self-esteem, and the realization of manhood he had never known before. Success for Doug was seeking first the kingdom of God, and a measure of real manhood followed.

Such a struggle. So well worth it.

The frustrations of the tensions between the two kingdoms, the struggle to balance the temporal and eternal, is only resolved when we seek first the eternal. Then all those things we seek in the temporal are added to us.

We erupt in praise to God when we realize who Christ is and the limitlessness He gives us. We see God as God when we meet Him all alone, stripped of all physical accoutrements and assets. We rise from our knees and stand strong, bringing the eternal to bear on the temporal. We don't shrink from adversity, neither do we ignore reality. Eternal hope transcends temporary circumstances. God through us conquers all.

Chapter 14
The Cost of Greatness

Maturity doesn't come with age, but begins with the acceptance of responsibility." I have made that statement more than once in meetings, and usually follow it with: "That's why some men are more mature at seventeen than others are at forty-seven." Once a woman on the front row burst out, "Forty-seven? You mean sixty-seven!"

True maturity and greatness in manhood begins with the acceptance of responsibility. You can see this in the epitome of the real man, Jesus. His greatness is viewed in light of the fact that He didn't just accept responsibility to come in the flesh in accordance with the Father's will, but that in redemption He accepted responsibility for the sins of all mankind.

To fulfill the Father's will, Christ bore the sins of the whole world at Calvary. It's one thing to accept responsibility for your own actions, another to accept those of the most profligate and reprehensible sinners, to bear their guilt and shame, and endure their punishment when you are completely innocent and guiltless. Add to that the cumulative wickedness of all mankind, and you inescapably conclude Jesus must be the Son of God to have borne such a burden. Most men can hardly bear their own guilt, much less take on that of the entire world.

Christ's greatness is intensified and glorified by His willingness to be the minister and servant of all mankind. He served men by becoming the Savior, offered redemption to all through His atonement at Calvary, and now serves humanity through meeting the needs of His church as their Intercessor, and answering the prayers of all who call on His Name.

Christ taught that "whoever desires to become great among you, let him be your servant. And whoever desires to be first among you, let him be your slave" (Matt. 20:26–27).

Greatness comes through serving. The more you serve, the greater you become.

Serving is not trying to compensate for what others didn't do. Serving involves meeting others' needs, through love, which is an expression of selflessness.

The Lord's greatness was seen when He took the towel to wash Peter's feet. Peter told Him he needed not only his feet, but his entire person washed. That is what Jesus really came to do, but in spirit, and what He was doing for Peter's feet was only a symbol of Jesus' ministry. His humility exemplified in such a servile act authenticated Christ's teaching as He taught not only in word but in example (John 13:1–17).

Jesus accepted the responsibility of serving. His own words still certify His ministry: "The Son of Man did not come to be served, but to serve" (Matt. 20:28). Due to His mercies, we daily exercise faith in Him, pray, and believe that He will answer. He has even charged the angels to be ministering spirits to those who will inherit salvation (Heb. 1:14). His benevolence knows no bounds, His grace no barrier, His love no end.

Billy Graham accepted the responsibility of serving as Christ's ambassador throughout the world. It meant growing into the responsibility personally, ministerially, culturally, spiritually, morally, and in his trustworthiness. Billy's greatness is apparent in the multitude to whom he has ministered and the longevity of his ministry.

Serving produces greatness in the world's system, as well as God's Kingdom. General Motors Corporation became one of the world's greatest companies because it served so many people. A small company in the beginning, it grew and generated greatness as it provided cars, equipment, and accessories.

Fame and greatness are not synonymous.

There is a vast difference between Madonna and Mother Teresa. Madonna is famous; Mother Teresa is great.

"Your care for others is the measure of your greatness," are the words of Jesus (Luke 9:48 LB).

The maturation process begins with faith, adds moral excellence, to that knowledge, then self-control, on to patience, developing godliness, brotherly kindness, and to all those—love (2 Peter 1:5–7). Initially, to begin the process, acceptance of responsibility for sin is necessary. The negative must be handled before positive progression can follow.

In a previous chapter, we talked about Eve succumbing to the three basic temptations in what is called the "original sin." Now let's look at Adam's part in it. God's directive to Adam was not to touch the fruit of the tree of life in the middle of the garden of Eden. Adam gave the commandment to Eve. The devil did not confront Adam, but deceived Eve into eating the fruit. Rationalizing his behavior to justify his action, Adam rejected God's will and word, and joined Eve in her insurrection (Gen. 3).

Later when Adam and Eve heard God's voice in the garden calling them to fellowship, they hid. When God confronted Adam, he admitted he was hiding due to his guilt and fear. God's next question was whether Adam had disobeyed Him and taken of the fruit.

Consider what Adam did at this point. God asked Adam a direct, confrontational question: "Did you take of the tree I told you not to?"

God was dealing with Adam as a Father to a son. Fathers confront their sons before meting out discipline, to teach their sons they must accept responsibility for their actions. Ordinarily the discipline fits the manner of responsibility shown. God wanted Adam to be a man. "Answer the question: Did you or didn't you?"

"The woman *You* gave me, she gave me of the tree and I did eat," Adam replied to the question.

Adam failed the test of manhood.

He blamed God for His trouble. Adam refused to accept responsibility for his actions.

Adam's reply set the course for men from then until now.

Some Bible scholars advocate that the reason for Adam's expulsion from Eden wasn't due to Adam's sin, but to his refusal to accept responsibility for his actions. They base this on the idea that God would have forgiven Adam if he had confessed, repented, and asked for forgiveness in integrity of heart. That he did not, made it impossible for God to leave him in the garden.

In Adam's sin against God, Adam's nature changed. The evidence was in his statement, "The woman whom You gave to be with me, she gave me of the tree, and I ate" (Gen. 3:12). Adam's accusation against God to justify himself displayed his complicity with Satan who is called the accuser of the brethren (Rev. 12:10). In Adam's accusation against God, he denied God's sovereignty. God's sovereignty exists in His absolute right to determine what is right and wrong for His creation, man.

God created Adam as a son. God dealt with Adam as with a son. When Adam sinned, the full revelation of the nature of God as a heavenly Father had to wait for the advent of another Adam, called God's "only begotten Son." Jesus as the "last Adam" brought the truth of God as Father, and through His Sonship enabled men to become sons of God by being born of God's Spirit as Christ was.

A basic tenet of fathering is teaching sons to accept responsibility for their actions. Discipline to enforce correction is one pattern to teach obedience. But before the father disciplines, he must make sure the son understands what is happening.

If a colonel on an Army base constantly tells his eight-year-old son not to play ball between the houses where they live, for fear of breaking a window, but a window is found broken, then before disciplining his son, the colonel asks his son if he did it. Many times a father will know a child has done something, but it is vital that the father give the child the opportunity to admit it so his child can accept responsibility for his own actions.

The discipline the son receives then becomes based on his honest admission of guilt. To lie, equivocate, deny, or pass blame on another to absolve himself would likely call for harsher punishment than an honest admission of disobedience. The father would be more pleased with the son's integrity and acceptance of responsibility than shirking it.

God is no different with His children. He expects us in our manhood to accept responsibility. Adam was the first man not to accept responsibility, but he certainly was not the last.

King David we know was a lover of truth and King Saul was not. Inseparably linked to the love of truth is the willingness to accept responsibility for what is true. When Saul was confronted with his sin of offering a sacrifice, usurping the priest's place, and not waiting for the prophet Samuel, Saul accused Samuel of being at fault because he did not arrive when Saul thought he should (1 Sam. 13:11). Saul's "forcing himself" to make the sacrifice offended God and his refusal to repent caused his rejection as king.

King David, on the other hand, grew in stature and in favor with

God and man. David took full responsibility for what God commanded him concerning Israel, her enemies, God's people, and his own actions. When the prophet Nathan confronted him about his adultery with Bathsheba, David repented in sackcloth and ashes (2 Sam. 12:16–17). Because he loved truth he applied it to his life.

In Ziklag, David's decisions and actions led to the capture of the families of his band of followers. It was the low point of his life. His own men, so loyal, steadfast in devotion, fighting to take him to the throne of Israel, were now talking of stoning him. Prayerful rather than prideful, David confessed his wrong decisions, sought God's forgiveness and mercy, and encouraged himself in the Lord. God then assured David that all the kidnapped families would be recovered. David's manhood, proven in crisis, brought the recovery of everything, including his stature in the sight of his men (1 Sam. 30:1–19).

The apostle Paul willingly took responsibility for the revelation of the Church, which God gave him while Paul was caught up in an exalted third heaven. Paul carried the fledgling young churches prayerfully in his heart and mind. He is the same one who confessed he was the "chiefest of sinners" and accepted responsibility for his violent actions against Christians before his conversion (1 Tim. 1:13). Paul accepted the responsibility of being a role model for every male believer in his day, saying, "Follow my example, as I follow the example of Christ" (1 Cor. 11:1 NIV). We still do.

Athletes who have fame and fortune as a result of their ability and prowess must accept the responsibility that it entails. Young men and women admire and emulate them. Refusing to accept responsibility as a role model for the young is simply disregarding societal duty.

Fathers who tell their children, "Don't do as I do, do as I say," are absolving themselves of responsibility to set a pattern of behavior for their children to imitate. Children may not always listen to you but they will always imitate you.

When a man finally accepts responsibility for his own actions it not only changes his destiny but that of others.

Jack King is a field representative for the Christian Men's Network. We work, pray, travel, and serve together all over the world. He came to the ministry with a remarkable testimony.

"Execution Style Murder" screamed the newspaper headlines

when Jack's father was found murdered by gun shots to the face. For years Jack carried a gun and spent most of his time planning to bring to justice the man who murdered his dad. A former U.S. Army Drill Sergeant, Jack had a rugged toughness that translated into a keen sense of hatred for the killer and a thirst for revenge. Worst of all, he believed he knew who the killer was—a business associate of his father's.

Then Jack was converted and Jesus Christ transformed his life, instantly releasing him from his intense hatred. But even as a recreated man, that hurt of his dad's murder lingered in his heart. One evening during a church service he heard God's Word that if he didn't forgive, God wouldn't forgive him. At that moment he prayed and asked God to forgive him for the hatred and murderous attitude he once had. He believed God heard and answered his prayer, but was unprepared for the immediate test God gave.

Only a few evenings later his wife asked him to go to the meat market from some ground beef. As he drove through the darkness he saw a commotion from a fire on the next street. As Jack drew closer, he recognized the location as the warehouse where he had found his murdered father, now owned by the man Jack had believed responsible for the execution.

Thinking to himself, "It serves him right," Jack continued on to the store. However a "small voice" told him he needed to go find that man and ask his forgiveness. When he left the store and started home he found he could not silence that inner voice and spontaneously turned down the other street to see if he could find his former enemy.

Getting out of his car at the spot where his father had died, Jack walked up the darkened alley to examine the chaos and see if he could find the business associate. In the flashing lights of the fire trucks, Jack saw another man standing in the darkness with him. Peering through the dark and smoke, Jack saw it was the very man he was after. Summoning every fiber of strength, he took a step toward him and asked, "Do you know me?"

"You look familiar," was the clipped reply.

"I'm Jack King."

Despite the darkness, Jack could see the man blanch with fear. Later Jack learned the man thought he had set the fire and now wanted to complete his revenge.

"God has changed my life," Jack told him, "and I've come to ask you to forgive me for accusing you of my dad's murder. I'm trying to make the things right that I did wrong before my conversion. One of the things I need to do is ask you to forgive me for my hatred and for haunting you these past few years. And for trying to ruin your life, your family, and your career."

"Yeah, well—" was the reply.

"Well, I want you to forgive me for all the harm I've done to you," Jack pressed. "Please forgive me."

"No problem. You're forgiven," the man said quickly, apparently wanting the conversation to end.

"No," Jack persisted, growing stronger with every word, "I mean really forgive me, not just in saying it, but in living it. I never want to offend you or hold ill-will against you again. I want you to know that."

There was a long pause. Finally the man let out a deep sigh and affirmed his forgiveness for Jack. Jack held out his hand and they shook on it.

With the awkwardness now over, Jack spent the next half hour telling his former enemy of how Christ had changed his life and what it meant to his family. The conversation ended with Jack praying the prayer of salvation with the man. Then Jack impulsively threw an arm around the man and the two wept on each other's shoulders as the years of hurt, hatred, and fear melted away.

On the way home Jack's tears were almost a hazard to his driving. The emotion-packed encounter had brought such release. Jack had the joy of knowing he had acted like a "real man." To this day Jack King is a new man. After all his "tough guy" days in football, the Army, and his career, Jack learned that accepting responsibility for his actions and making restitution gave him a sense of manhood not found anywhere else.

God never asked Jack to take on the responsibility of his father's murder. God is taking care of that. " 'Vengeance is Mine, I will repay,' says the Lord" (Rom. 12:19). Jack's responsibility was to have a pure heart, full of forgiveness toward others, so God would fully forgive him.

Individually or corporately, being responsible determines greatness of life.

Our fame, fortune, prestige, or power don't tell the tale; the manner in which we serve does. And that is built on the responsibility we're willing to accept. "Whoever desires to be first among you, let him be your servant" (Matt. 20:26) is the Word of Him who serves as Savior and Lord.

Chapter 15
The Winning Strategy

Knowledge is the acquiring of facts, understanding is the interpreting of facts, wisdom the application. Of these three, wisdom is so vital that God calls it the "principal thing" (Prov. 4:7). There is no area in life that does not benefit from wisdom.

God admonishes us to ask Him for wisdom, and promises to give it generously without finding fault, or looking for an excuse not to answer our request (James 1:5). When Solomon succeeded David as king, the Lord visited Solomon in a dream and asked what He could give him. Solomon asked for discernment in judging the people. Solomon's request so pleased God that He promised him riches and honor unequaled in all history, plus a wise and discerning heart (1 Kings 3:4–9).

There are two kinds of wisdom mentioned in the Bible. *Divine* wisdom comes "from above" and is "first pure, then peaceable, gentle, willing to yield, full of mercy and good fruits, without partiality and without hypocrisy" (James 3:17). The characteristics of this kind of wisdom stem from the character of God. The other kind is "earthly, sensual, demonic" (James 3:15). The results of having godly wisdom are a long good life, riches, honor, pleasure, and peace (Prov. 3:16–17). Godly wisdom provides for a man's total needs.

The prerequisite for acquiring godly wisdom is fear of the Lord. "The fear of the LORD is the beginning of wisdom" (Ps. 111:10). This is true because when we fear the Lord we flee iniquity, which is wise living. The fear of the Lord is a reverent awe of God, and causes a hatred of evil. It means to acknowledge God for Who He is, in all His power and majesty.

Solomon illustrated his fear of God before he asked for wisdom. He pointed out his recognition that God was the Creator, the One who gave him his life and kingdom, and the God of the people he ruled.

> You have shown great mercy to your servant David my father, be-
> cause he walked before You in truth, in righteousness, and in up-
> rightness of heart with You; You have continued this great kindness
> for him, and You have given him a son to sit on his throne, as it is
> this day. Now, O LORD my God, You have made Your servant king.
> (1 Kings 3:6–8)

Because of his fear of the Lord, God granted his request for wisdom and then some.

Adam, as the first man, was given a spirit of wisdom. He lost the
fear of the Lord and sinned, and as a result his wisdom was blighted.
Jesus came as the Last Adam, a man who once again had the "Spirit
of wisdom and understanding" (Isa. 11:2). Through Him, that wisdom is available to us. The Bible teaches that Jesus "became for us
wisdom" (1 Cor. 1:30). Through Christ, God freely gives us wisdom
(James 1:5). It is Christ who enables us to know the manifest wisdom
of God (Eph. 3:10).

People who reject Christ are left with only human wisdom which
is "earthly," "sensual," and "devilish." By their rejection of the fear of
the Lord, they reject true wisdom (Prov. 1:29–31). The Bible calls
them fools (Prov. 1:7, 23:9).

Look at some of the ways wisdom is applied in our lives. It is basic
wisdom to prepare for the future and foolishness not to. Jesus illustrated this with a story about a man who was to be discharged from a
management position. Concerned about his future, he discounted
each creditor's account before he left the firm. His strategy was to
find favor with one of them so he would employ him when he was
fired (Luke 16:1–8). Jesus commended the man, not for his chica-
nery, but for the basic wisdom he used to secure his future.

We often flunk the basics. Failing to prepare for a future in this life
through dropping out of school is one thing, to flunk the course that
prepares for discharge from this life by rejecting the Bible is another.
If a man knows that one day he is going to be discharged from this
life, failure to prepare for what comes next is foolish. A man plays the
fool by failing to study in school, and failing to study God's Word.

It is wisdom to heed the principle "First in intention is last in execution." For example, on a recent trip I planned to go to Brisbane,

Perth, and Sydney, Australia. That was my first in intention. However, I had to arrange for a visa, buy tickets, pack bags, arrange travel, coordinate personnel, fly there, and finally arrive—my first intention was the last thing I executed.

Most people begin planning for big events with "first things first." It is wisdom to begin planning what occurs after the event, then working back to the present. Too often people plan for meetings, weddings, special events, starting at the beginning only to come to the end and ask for volunteers to help clean up or pack—often doing it all themselves because of faulty planning.

The first intention in any life is to go to heaven, but it is the last thing that is done. Everything between then and now is just a preparation for that event. From now until you arrive there, you continue with life's plan to make it happen.

The famous basketball coach John Wooden put it: "Failure to prepare is preparation for failure." True in sport. True in life and death. This is basic wisdom.

Consider what happens to those without wisdom. Satan has no wisdom. He has knowledge but lacks true wisdom because he has no fear of the Lord. When Satan lost his fear of the Lord and was cast out of heaven, he lost his wisdom (Ezek. 28:14–16). Therefore, the man who has godly wisdom has dominion over the devil. The man who has earthly wisdom invites the devil and the world to exercise dominion over him.

All sin is a form of insanity. Satan is the most insane being of all because he still believes he can defeat God.

Those who succumb to his temptations adopt behaviors that are utterly unreasonable and therefore, technically insane.

Doug Stringer is a young minister who started on the streets of Houston and now has a network of outreaches all over the world. He sent me a video recently with interviews of young men who practice homosexuality in the inner city of Houston. Teenaged men said on-camera that they continued in their promiscuity even though they knew some of the their partners might have AIDS. An AIDS sufferer said on-camera, "I only wish I could tell them what it is like—the trauma, terror, suffering—and warn them to stop before it is too late."

We fall prey to the insanity of sin—at times even shocking ourselves.

I was counseling a man who had committed adultery but was now reconciling with his wife. Nancy and I took them to lunch one day and ended up talking about his affair. His wife turned to him and asked, "Didn't you think of me or the children when you were doing it?"

He shook his head and said seriously, "The only thing I thought of was my own pleasure."

Remember, sin never thinks of the consequences, only the pleasure of the moment. This man never intended to hurt his wife or estrange his children. To do so was beyond reason. He loved them, but did it anyhow.

God's strategy to deliver men from their folly is Calvary. There Jesus made the sacrifice so that every man could be changed eternally and take dominion over sin, Satan, and even death. Once we accept that sacrifice, we are candidates for receiving God's wisdom.

God's wisdom, in turn, is the key to gaining victory in almost every area of life. Think of wisdom in practical terms, as it relates to your marriage, business decisions, financial problems or health. Wisdom is really the key to every problem confronting you.

One day as I was reading the prayer requests people send me, I couldn't help but notice how often they used the word, "victory." They needed to overcome behaviors, difficulties, and afflictions in various areas of their lives, but referred to it all colloquially as wanting "victory."

It occurred to me that the word *victory* was a miscellaneous noun used to describe the solution to any need. "Victory in marriage" meant they wanted to reconcile with their separated mate. "Victory over finances" meant they wanted to get out of debt. "Victory in health" meant they wanted to be cured of something. They all wanted "victory."

Victory is always glorious, and it is the glory of the victory they really desire. God gives grace to sinners, but glory to saints. Believers are being changed "from glory to glory" (2 Cor. 3:18).

To have glory a victory is needed; to obtain victory a strategy is required; to acquire strategy wisdom is necessary. Instead of asking for "victory," these people needed to seek the prerequisite—wisdom. God's wisdom will give them a strategy to obtain the victory so they can enjoy the glory.

The glory is in the victory, but the wisdom is in the strategy.

Scripture tells of the Syrian General Naaman who desperately sought a cure for his leprosy, and when it was proffered almost missed it, by refusing the strategy necessary to be healed. A servant maid, carried captive to Syria from Israel, spoke to her mistress, the wife of Naaman, and suggested that Naaman go to the prophet in Israel to be healed. Naaman went carrying jewels, money, and clothes to give the seer as a gesture of payment for his recovery. When Naaman arrived at the prophet's home, the prophet didn't bother to meet Naaman, but sent his servant to tell him to dip in the Jordan River seven times. Naaman was incensed that the prophet would not meet him in person, but was simply told by a servant to dip in a muddy river. His pride suffered an indignity.

"I thought at least he would come out and talk to me! I expected him to wave his hand over the leprosy and call upon the name of the Lord his God, and heal me!" Naaman said (2 Kings 5:11 LB).

As he started to leave, filled with umbrage at the insult, one of his menial servants said, "If the prophet had told you to do some great thing, wouldn't you have done it? So you should certainly obey him when he says simply to go and wash and be cured" (2 Kings 5:13 LB).

Those words halted Naaman. He considered the words of the servant, obeyed the command of the prophet, and was miraculously healed after his obedience.

The barriers Naaman had to overcome in himself were the same that you and I stumble over: predisposition, predetermination, and preconception. We imagine when our victory will occur, and how it will happen. But when the strategy is not what we envisioned it to be, we have a difficult time accepting it and can miss God's wisdom.

Naaman was actually guilty of "magical thinking." God is a miracle worker, not a magician.

In a meeting one evening a man involved in "magical thinking" requested me to pray for his marriage. For twenty-five years he had taken his wife for granted, allowed himself to become careless in manner and dress, and failed to provide for his family's needs. Meantime, his wife took care of the family, finished her education, established a career, and finally with hopelessness for him, filed for divorce. Suddenly desperate, he wanted someone to pray over him and heal him of twenty-five years of poor stewardship in his marriage. He wanted to erase instantly by some magical process in prayer a quarter century of slack and sloth he had put into the marriage. Of course God will resurrect marriages, but He does it through the applied obedience of the individual, not by magic.

Remember, no man possesses his wife in marriage, he is only a steward of her love. He must prove himself a good steward of that love to maintain it over the years. I did pray for this man, but I also gave him a little wisdom.

"A man may ruin his chances by his own foolishness and then blame it on the Lord" (Prov. 19:3 LB).

In the world of sports, the God-given pattern of wisdom for victory is always used. Applied knowledge translates into wisdom which develops strategies which ensure victories. Sounds complex, but every great athlete knows it. Take what you know, apply it with wisdom to develop a strategy, and you win!

I heard a story years ago and never forgot it. Here's how I remember it: Amos Alonzo Stagg was an all-time great football coach. While coaching from a wheelchair, a reporter told him, "You know more about football than any man alive. That must be why your team wins so much."

"You're wrong," said the venerable sportsman. "It's not what I know that wins games, it's what those young men on the field know." In his coaching, to teach what he knew, Stagg understood that execution wins games, and execution comes from practice, and practice is doing what you were taught until you excel at it.

We men are naturally drawn to such victories. We are attracted by winners, which is why we like reading the sports pages of the newspaper. The sports page has winners, the front page has losers. The thrill of victory is the glory that it brings. When a football team leaves a field victoriously, the locker room becomes charged with the atmosphere of a winner. Men revel in the glory of the "win." They revel in "victory" and "success" because there is glory in victory.

It's the glory we desire, not just the victory. Wisdom—strategy—victory—glory. God's pattern.

Failures can have purpose, and even a reward of sorts, but winning is always glorious. Winning teams, political parties, and game show contestants erupt in delirious celebration when victory occurs. Even conservative golfers, scientists, and businessmen shed tears of joy on the day of their greatest feats.

Christian men and women pray for "victories" in their lives because they want to experience the glory of the win. The Bible teaches us to "glory in the Lord" (1 Cor. 1:31). God wants us to be victorious and go "from glory to glory." No wonder He wants to give us wisdom. Since the glory is in the victory, to go from "glory to glory" we must go from "victory to victory."

Victory is revealed in public, but is developed in private. Only victors know the hard, long, lonely, bruising hours they experience all alone with only their desire. When a man wins the decathlon, or a young girl excels in gymnastics, none know better than they the rigors required. Too often the difference between winning and losing is in hundredths of a second or fractions of an inch. A wise man disciplines himself in developing a strategy to accomplish such a small thing. The constant pays off in the instant. Strategies are developed in private, victories are won in public.

Parenting, business, sports, investments, friendships, purchases, marriages—we need wisdom for them all.

Jared is now a friend of mine. One night he was high on crystal-meth when his mother visited and left him a little book called *Courage*.[1] Jared's wife had just left him and taken their new baby with her. He was alone. He had no money. He couldn't shake his craving for drugs. That night, even through drug-induced euphoria, he became overwhelmed with despair. He picked up the book and read it until the early morning hours.

When he finished, Jared told God that if He was real, to save him. Then he miraculously fell asleep, even while "high." Jared awoke at almost noon the next day completely sober. His drive for drugs was gone and he was hungry to read God's Word. How it happened he doesn't know, outside of a complete miracle of God. Only rarely have I heard of God so miraculously delivering someone, without his facing the grim realities of detoxification and withdrawal.

Still, Jared's marriage was ruined beyond repair. Selfishness, a bad disposition, poor work stability, and then spending her carefully saved Christmas money on drugs finally caused her to leave in disgust. She wanted nothing to do with him, took legal action to keep him away, and was trying to finalize a divorce as quickly as she could.

Realizing he needed God's wisdom and a strategy to restore the marriage, Jared seriously, daily, sought God's wisdom. He found it when he learned that if you have left your first love you need to go back and do your "first works" again (Rev. 2:5). He began by writing letters of repentance and apology to his wife, asking for forgiveness, and telling her of a newfound love for her. He worked in a lumberyard and was not flush with income, but the money he made was no longer being consumed by drugs. With what he saved, Jared lavished her with gifts. At times he would take roses by her house and leave them on her windshield at four in the morning, so she would have them when she left for work.

Eventually she agreed to see him once, *if* he repaired a wall he had put a fist through before he left. After that she agreed to go with him to a counselor. Attending those sessions, then enjoying each other's company after, her cold heart began to thaw and the truth of Jared's changed life and love for her melted her resolve.

The day came when he proposed and surprised her with a ring and clothes for a second wedding. She accepted. I had the pleasure of performing the renewal of their vows on the jetty at the beach. It was a beautiful morning, and they were truly in love all over again.

But Jared had one more surprise for her. He had made a down payment on a home, her first. When they left the beach that day he drove her to the new home that had been one of her greatest dreams. He embraced her dream as his own by his provision.

God-given dreams, in God-favored men, make a God-blessed world.[2]

Management seminars will teach you, "Extreme situations call for extreme actions." Jared made extreme use of godly wisdom and has a new home and family to show for it. Not just that, but after his faithfulness at the lumberyard, he recently traded his coveralls for a suit and tie in a management position.

A lesser man would have acknowledged his need for help, but prayed for an instantaneous solution like the drug deliverance, instead of seeking and acting on wisdom. With the strategy obtained, Jared will be able to maintain a victorious marriage long after the honeymoon is over.

Levels of knowledge begin at the bottom with assumption, then knowledge, skill, and practice. The issue is not whether you have the knowledge to employ the skill to do something once, but whether or not you put it into practice. A lucky golfer may break par once, but a successful player does it successively because he has made it a practice.

The value of wisdom is "better than rubies," and its worth exceeds that of gold or silver (Prov. 8:11). God does not give wisdom to the casual, slothful, indifferent, or superficial inquirer. He reveals wisdom only to those who realize its value, seek it wholeheartedly, earnestly desire it, and value it as the priceless "gift" it really is.

God has promised to give wisdom, but says we must seek it first.

> If you seek her as silver,
> And search for her as for hidden treasures;
> Then you will understand the fear of the LORD,
> And find the knowledge of God.
> For the LORD gives wisdom;
> From His mouth come knowledge and understanding.
> (Prov. 2:4–6)

Wisdom lies below the surface of knowledge. You have to dig for it, but the effort is worth the reward.

Chapter 16
Employed for Life

I was chatting with a pastor friend of mine at a banquet when he told me something that jarred me. I suddenly realized he was teaching me a principle which, if not understood, robs a man of a measure of dignity. In a nutshell, he said that employment, both in the secular and sacred fields, creates production and momentum, but unemployment creates a stifling atmosphere. The principles he developed from that thought had helped his church grow and had inspired and motivated him and his congregation. Added to thoughts of my own and others, the truth has become vital to me and is relevant to all who desire fulfillment and satisfaction in life.

Another minister friend has stated that "all truth is parallel."[1] What is found in the eternal has a parallel in the temporal. This is similar to what we have already established in "seeking first the kingdom of God," and having temporal "things" follow. When something is happening in one realm, there is a parallel in the other.

Rob Carman, a pastor in Albuquerque, is the friend who discovered through a series of events this connection between that in the secular and that in the sacred realms. His congregation had reached a certain plateau numerically after starting with a handful of people and growing to a population of approximately 1,500. The zeal, fervor, and aggressiveness that had characterized the initial growth seemed to have lost its momentum. Personally, the time he had formerly had for prayer and study now seemed to have been usurped by an increased schedule of counseling, moral issues being contested among members, and a plethora of family problems.

Perplexed and distressed by it, and in deep concern over the situation, he was meditating in the Scriptures one day when he remembered an article he had seen in the newspaper days before. He recalled seeing a report citing statistics of what happens to a community when unemployment rises. He realized that what happened in the community at large was similar to what he was experiencing in the community of the church. As he pondered the thought, the parallel became apparent.

The report stated that the effects of high unemployment cause primarily and fundamentally the loss of self-esteem in men. When a man cannot provide for himself or his own he is robbed of his dignity. That loss affects the individual, his family, and society in general. The resulting societal evils, including drugs, promiscuity, disease, and welfare abuse, are a plague on its people. The bulk of the citizenry and its leaders are required to meet the needs for counsel, medication, and social assistance.

At the root of the problem lies the fact that men were created in the image of God, were given abilities and creativity, and required to produce. When a man's abilities and creativity are stifled through unemployment and cannot be used in gainful productivity, he will find a way to express them. If they cannot be expressed legally, he will find fulfillment illegally, immorally, and illicitly.

Rob explained it this way, "When a man is robbed of his right to work, to earn an honest dollar for an honest day's work, he is robbed of his right to use his ability and is made dependent on a system that violates him." In Third World nations and neighborhood ghettos around the world, where there is exaggerated unemployment, when worth and self-esteem are taken from men, they move into illegal or immoral activities to satisfy and fulfill themselves.

Today, government agencies admit that drug dealing will never be stopped by merely legal methods. When a teenager pushing drugs walks down the street with money stuffed in his pockets, his value as a man has been gratified to a great extent. His gratification in his ability to earn money, in exercising his creativity to obtain it, and in the productivity of making it satisfies his manhood. His method is morally and legally wrong, but nevertheless, he feels fulfilled.

The Bible lays down a work ethic for all society which says if you don't work, you don't eat (2 Thess. 3:10). The simple reason for the work ethic is the dignity of man. When God gave manna in the wilderness, He could have given it a month at a time. Instead, He gave it on a daily basis so work was provided and dignity was given. Without working for what he is eating, a man is living off someone else's dignity.

In reference to Satan, Jesus taught that the thief comes to steal, kill, and destroy (John 10:10). Stealing ability, killing creativity, destroying productivity is devilish.

America today is in danger of destruction, not from its enemies, but due to shifting from a productive society to a consumer-oriented society. The nation has shifted from a position of wealth and strength to become the world's largest debtor nation. "Japan bashing" is in vogue because of Japan's financial power in America, and the world, but the truth is that Japan has simply out-produced the U.S. The Japanese work ethic is as strong as or stronger than ever, while the work ethic in America is almost in eclipse.

In other countries, socialism teaches men to depend on the system to provide for them. They come to depend on authorities to give them benevolence from taxes exacted from them, and even worse, in totalitarian nations, dictators assume divine status in their own eyes, and promulgate that to their citizens. How can governmental leaders give that which they have not first taken? Socialism in all its forms is a proven failure. In New Zealand, where the Christian Men's Network enjoys a thriving ministry among the churches, their "dole" system has almost crippled the entire country. Communism, another failure, was a feudal system. Party bosses were lords and citizens simply serfs.

The welfare system in America is a type of socialism. What started idealistically as a way to free people from "poor farms" has enslaved those it meant to save. The "poor farm," where families were sent to live until work was available, became a symbol for failure, and those using it were considered second- or third-class citizens. Welfare was established to replace the farms and was simply meant to be a temporary help until those helped could become productive again. But today, rather than using welfare to provide a place for people to prepare for work, many recipients make more on welfare than working for minimum wage, so are robbed of a reason to go to work and be productive. The result is mentally and morally emasculated manhood. The welfare system is much-derided because experts say it teaches people to violate the program to provide for themselves, and in some cities, such as New York, it saps the very vitality of the city's economy. Exacerbating the city's financial plight, the results are thoroughfares with unrepaired potholes, garbage and trash littering streets and vacant lots, graffiti disgracing vehicles and buildings, and indifference to the blight by elected officials.

High unemployment creates compound difficulties that require more than the tax-paying citizenry can pay for, or its leaders can supply. Unemployment of 25 percent in communities is considered excessive, propagates the problems and distresses just talked about, and perpetuates a "poverty complex."

This is the secular side of it, but a parallel is in the sacred. Consider the estimates that rate between 75–80 percent of church members as only "hearers" but not "doers" in the church. These are people who want the church to support them rather than them support the church, and make the church conduct itself in a form of "spiritual socialism." Its adherents have a "welfare mentality" that depends on the pastor as the source of all wisdom and the church program to maintain them. In such cases, the pastor, not the Bible, becomes the source of faith and the rule for their conduct.

Being without the fulfillment and satisfaction gained from service to the Lord, church members are robbed of their true value to the kingdom of God, and commonly turn to things illicit, immoral, or illegal to provide for the void in their lives.

In the competition between the church and world, the world wins when the church cannot provide the quickening power of the Holy Spirit to make alive the reality of the gospel, the joy of worship, the dynamism of preaching, the wonder of answered prayer, the "anointed high" from sharing truth, or the splendor of fellowship with Jesus. Sterile sermons cannot compete with the crap tables in casinos. Pathetic prayers don't have the exhilaration of pornography. Boring church rituals are no match for football or baseball. Faked smiles at church socials don't have the dynamism of a rock concert.

Spiritually unemployed Christians have "religion" that offers them none of the excitement of living that the spiritually employed enjoy. By definition, the spiritually employed are those men (and women) who have found the reality of a vital living relationship with Jesus Christ, become a partaker of His Spirit, been made alive through His indwelling life, and have submitted themselves to His Word and will. Enlisted in an army of those desiring to fulfill His commission to "make disciples" of those who have never known Him, they are actively engaged in serving, exercising those "serving gifts" Christ gives to men, and finding fulfillment and satisfaction of the highest order.

When such people attend church services they are eager to learn, hungry to digest truth, delighted in worship, and discover new joys in helping others. Their desire is to see others share the same relationship with the Lord Jesus Christ they have discovered and experienced.

Conversely, if estimates are correct, most people attend church meetings to "be blessed," not to "be a blessing." Selfishly desiring only what benefits them, wanting only their own blessing, they become easily dissatisfied when things don't satisfy them or meet their expectations. Perhaps the pastor's message isn't up to standard, the music isn't suiting, ushers aren't polite, and when things aren't pleasing to them they leave disgruntled and unhappy. However when people arrive with the attitude of serving God, worshiping Christ, ministering to the Lord and His church, they leave blessed no matter what happens.

It's the 80–20 principle at work. Businessmen realize that 20 percent of their clients provide 80 percent of their work. School teachers know that 20 percent of the students create 80 percent of the problems. And pastors know that approximately 20 percent of the people do 80 percent of the work of the church. The rest are spiritually unemployed. In the void of productivity, they become more of a problem than a solution. Such an exaggerated rate means the excitement, zeal, and fervor of serving God is dreadfully diminished, and means to provide the zest for life is found other than in the church and the Lord's service.

At a recent Christian Men's Event in Southern California, some young teen-men stood to tell what they found exciting about the life they were living. Standing before the audience with their hair pulled back tightly and bound with a net, pegged pants, necklace chains, and inscribed T-shirts, holding the biggest Bibles they could find, each in turn told the hundreds of men there that they had formerly been gang members, running with guns and knives, but since becoming Christians have found the most exciting life of all. In short speeches punctuated with Scriptures recited from memory, these young men charged the crowd with their enthusiasm, telling of their daring to go back to the gangs and share the life of Christ.

"There is no high like the spiritual high that Jesus gives," one of them said. "The guys I used to run around with stopped running with me. When I had a gun and knife, nobody was afraid of me, but since I found Jesus and try to tell them about Him, they are all afraid of me. Nobody wants to get in my car with me now because they're afraid I'll try to convert them. And I will!"

These young men are filled with excitement for the Lord, busy about the the Lord's business, and no longer have time for things illicit, immoral, or illegal. They are spiritually employed in the greatest work on earth.

And they're right—there is no "high" like that which comes from praying with or for someone who is helped eternally. Nothing can substitute for the thrill of seeing someone experience a newfound relationship with Jesus Christ.

The apostle Paul gave Timothy a simple instruction that applies to all believers: "But you be watchful in all things, endure afflictions, do the work of an evangelist, fulfill your ministry" (2 Tim. 4:5).

If this were a job description for Billy Graham, it might have said, "Be an evangelist." But Paul worded it differently: "Do the work of an evangelist." He commands all of us to tell people about Jesus to "fulfill" our ministry. What does it mean to "fulfill" our ministry? People who are physically unemployed may go to seminars or read books to find where they fit in the job market, but God's Kingdom doesn't work that way. The Christlike don't discover their ministry gifts by sitting around analyzing someone else's teaching. Gifts are determined as they become manifest in the process of ministering to others. During the course of ministry a person's gifts are manifested. By doing the work of an evangelist, the Spirit of God manifests our ministry and motivational gifts, and brings us the realization of our temperament.

Inactivity produces nothing. When actively pursuing truth in word and deed, productivity results.

Reading the Bible is being spiritually employed. Praying with your wife is being spiritually employed. So is sharing your faith with another, visiting the sick and lonely, and most of all, doing something to help another know Christ. Doing the work of an evangelist is vital.

Evangelistic work develops a pattern for life that necessitates a vital prayer life, boldness in identity with Christ, and finding commonality with others in order to share with them. Men must see the necessity of the Kingdom harvest to retain

- the value of their own personal salvation,
- the true meaning of Calvary,
- a hunger for God's Word,
- a desire for God's reward,
- the purpose of the Holy Spirit in life,
- the reason for being a Christian,
- to keep sight of eternity, and
- maintain faithful stewardship of life.

These attributes all naturally spring from evangelism.

When Rob Carman learned this principle and began to teach it to his congregation, as many as 92 percent of the members became spiritually employed in some kind of evangelistic work. They began testifying, witnessing to acquaintances and friends, or to strangers on street corners, depending on their ministry gifts, and began encouraging other Christians in home groups. In one year those church members ministered individually to 150,000 people. That's employment!

The pastor no longer was looked to for the resolution of every problem because they began to study the Bible. He was free to return to his Bible study, praying, and preaching. They all, pastor and people, started reaping earthly benefits of their employment—a sense of self-worth and dignity that came as a result of carrying out God's plan by being creative and productive.

When people become spiritually employed, the kingdom of God on earth is released. To a real man, spiritual employment brings dignity, prosperity, authority, charity, and tranquility.

"Therefore, my beloved brethren, be steadfast, immovable, always abounding in the work of the Lord, knowing that your labor is not in vain in the Lord" (1 Cor. 15:58).

Chapter 17
Financial Freedom

Carman called me late one evening when we were both in hotels, only he was thousands of miles from me. He was troubled by an earlier conversation he had with a friend.

Carman is more than a gospel singer in my estimation. He is a qualified musical genius. He has raised the art of storytelling in music to a new form. Drama, staging, sound, melody, and lyric combine in a presentation that is unique in the world. His is a blend of truth in song that impacts men and women, especially the young, and attracts them by the multiplied thousands to his concerts. He broke records and attracted the secular media with his 20,000-member audience in Detroit. "Sold out" is an understatement. You need to arrive hours early to think of getting a seat when he ministers. For this incredibly gifted and dedicated young man to be troubled by anything drew my immediate attention and concern.

A friend had chided Carman for using his talented gift for the "gospel circuit" instead of taking it into the arena of Hollywood and pop music. His friend contended Carman could become famous and rich, win Grammys, and later in life do something for the Lord "after making a name for himself."

"Why waste your talent?" was the question Carman's friend asked.

"Ed, I don't want to waste my talent," Carman told me.

His friend said that he was in Hollywood to make it "big," and then when famous use his influence for the Lord. The friend thought that was better than taking the best years of life and spending them traveling and ministering the Gospel where there isn't much money or fame.

As we talked, Carman answered his own question as he asked it saying, "To me, a waste is taking the best of what you have and using it on the devil's work, then giving what you have left to the Lord," he concluded.

"You're absolutely right!" I emphatically assured him.

Investing your energy, ingenuity, initiative, ability, and creativity in the kingdom of God is wisdom, not waste. Carman is only one of the new breed of men who are coming to the front today, bringing their influence for good into this desperately needy world.

Giving to God is never a waste. When we give money to God in an offering, we give for many different reasons but we always give to Him, not to the man taking the offering. By our giving we gain something that is impossible to gain any other way. The benefits of giving are great, but often the use of money is the acid test of character in a real man.

The worldly attitude and philosophy of Carman's friend is something people have believed for years, thinking that to give God their best somehow robs them of what is best for them. Nothing could be further from the truth. Giving to God brings His favor through obedience and is worth more than anything anyone could ever buy or gain.

Israel battled this attitude. At first, when God brought the Israelites out of Egypt's bondage, their gratitude knew no bounds. When Moses told them they were to build a tabernacle in the wilderness, their offerings were so generous he had to restrain them from giving more. They laid their lives and all they possessed on the Lord's altar in worship (Exod. 35).

But centuries later the prophet Malachi thundered an indictment from God to the children of those previous generations. Once generous to a fault, they were now bringing the sick, weak, and maimed of their flocks and herds to offer on the altar. They still had the external accoutrements of their worship, but had lost the internal power of God's presence. Because of it, they kept the best for themselves, reinvesting it in their worldly business, and gave the leftovers to God.

"Offer that to your governor and see what he will do about it," God said through Malachi. "If then I am the Father, / Where is My honor?" (Mal. 1:6).

Their miserly offerings were a dishonor to Jehovah God, their Savior and Deliverer. They were a young generation who never knew Egypt or the miracles God performed to set their fathers free from slavery. As their hearts hardened toward Him, they saw nothing wrong with giving God the leftovers of their possessions and keeping the best for themselves. The real waste was their whole lives.

Giving God the dregs of life is shameful, selfish, and sinful. Giving yourself to God is your greatest honor.

Jesus taught a parable about a Pharisee who prayed self-righteously in public and a publican who prayed humbly in private. The Pharisee in his self-righteousness had little to give but much to boast about, while the publican had nothing to boast about and could only give himself. Jesus said the publican left justified, while the Pharisee didn't (Luke 18:9–14).

When Jesus was in the house of Simon the leper, a woman with an alabaster box came and showered its priceless contents upon Jesus, anointing His feet and wiping them with her hair. She was lavishing herself and her most precious possession on her Lord. Some of His disciples began to complain saying, "To what purpose is this waste? For this fragrant oil might have been sold for much and given to the poor" (Matt. 26:8–9). John records this statement as coming from Judas who held the purse with the money (John 12:5–6). Like many treasurers, Judas became ego-identified with the money, developed a possessive attitude toward it, and his covetousness later motivated him to negotiate the betrayal of Jesus for profit, a profit he never realized because the bitterness of betrayal turned him to suicide. The irony is that Judas protested, what he considered, the waste of priceless possessions on Christ, but wasted his own most precious possession—his life.

The Lord answered his disciples that day by reminding them: "For you have the poor with you always, but Me you do not have always" (Matt. 26:11).

When Robert Schuller built the Crystal Cathedral, carping critics said the money would be better spent caring for the poor and homeless. Yet if all the money spent on the Cathedral was used to help the poor and homeless, we would still have as many or more of the poor and homeless to care for today, but not the beautiful monument to the glory of God. Yet how many men throughout the world have been attracted to the Gospel through the Cathedral, and how many have been transformed and strengthened through his ministry over the years?

Giving your best to God is not a waste—it is a glory! Jesus taught that when you have the opportunity to do something that will glorify God, do it. God is worthy of our very best, and He requires it.

Many drama critics have never produced a play. Many sports writers who criticize athletes have never played the game. Most columnists who second guess politicians have never run for office. In the same way, most of those who criticize the Gospel have never attempted to do God service. Generally speaking it is the story of the have-nots finding fault with the haves. So don't let some critic keep you from giving your best to God. It would be your loss, not his. Don't let someone's faultfinding become your stumbling block.

When Jesus taught about the deceitfulness of riches, He didn't discourage riches nor condemn those who were rich. He taught the deceit of riches as (1) the tendency to trust in them instead of God; (2) being deceived into thinking riches bring happiness and health; and (3) being seduced by thinking no matter how much you have it is never enough. The real man doesn't rely on riches, but on God; doesn't expect happiness from riches, but from friendships; doesn't crave more, but finds that "godliness with contentment is great gain" (1 Tim. 6:6).

Without being caught in the deceitfulness of riches we can be focused on generosity, knowing that Jesus gave all, even His very life. Through His example, we know liberality is a mark of largeness in manhood. A man reveals the condition of his heart by his attitude toward money. No wonder Jesus sat in temples watching people give their offerings. "Where your treasure is, there your heart will be also" (Matt. 6:21).

Our attitude in giving is sure to be tested. I received a very official-looking letter from someone who invited me to join in a class-action suit to recover monies from Jim Bakker and the defunct PTL Ministries. Nancy and I had given monies to the ministry and invested in a "time share" program because we enjoyed the Christian family atmosphere. Their camp-like retreat center in North Carolina was simply a glorified campground similar to what we knew when we summered at "Camp Meetings."

Now I was asked to sue Jim Bakker to recover the monies I had given and invested. I showed the letter to Nancy and we agreed to throw it away. When we invested in that ministry, we gave to God, not Jim. If I were to sue for recovery I would have to sue God!

Nothing lavished on Jesus is ever wasted. Whatever is given will always have a return. God is debtor to no man; therefore, no man can put God in his debt (Ps. 50:12–15). The Lord always gives more in return which keeps Him from becoming a debtor to any man. This frees men to give liberally (Luke 6:38), knowing they cannot outgive God.

Contributing money to ministries is a joy, but in giving we understand the offering is to God, and that any blessing or return benefit will come from God, not man.

I learned my lesson years ago. A pastor friend named Gerald and I were crossing the Puget Sound on a ferry, going from his hometown of Port Orchard to Seattle, to attend a gathering of men and ministers. In the throes of the final week of a forty-day fast, sensitive to God's Spirit, I felt a strong urge to give Gerald the one hundred dollars in my billfold. It was the only money I had. With the action came a surge of well-being, expansiveness, completeness, from both the obedience of the act and from the generous nature of it. I felt a great sense of accomplishment in my obedience.

Going home from the meeting, Gerald said, "Ed, it's good you gave me that hundred because I gave it to the minister in the meeting who fell off his ladder, broke his arm, and didn't have money for doctor bills. I figured he needed it more than I did."

As he spoke, I became upset with him. No, I was mad. That was my last hundred, and when I gave it to him, I never expected he would give it away. My expansiveness, well-being, completeness shrank to nothing because he gave my money away. How dare he?

About the time I thought all this, I heard the still small voice of the Holy Spirit in my mind and heart bringing me the words of Jesus.

"Did I tell you to give it?" He asked.

"Yes, Lord," I answered in my mind.

"Did you give it to Me?"

"Yes, Lord."

"Your reward is in your obedience to Me and does not rest on what others do with what I tell you to give."

Okay, that was it. Once given—out of my control.

From that moment to this, I have never worried concerning contributions. I don't worry about what others do with what I give. At times I even give with the smallest urging to those I am not sure will deal righteously with my gift. They will give an account to God for their disposition of the monies, not to me.

Just because some bankers are guilty of fraud doesn't stop me from banking my money. Some of my tax money may find its way into someone's pocket, but I don't quit paying taxes. And though there may be ministers who have used the gifts of God's people lustfully, selfishly, and personally, that doesn't stop me from giving to God. My responsibility to God is not built on someone else's relationship to Him, although I don't deliberately set out to give irresponsibly, capriciously, or carelessly, but responsibly and liberally as pleasing to God.

Tithes are the monies we give God before offerings. The tithe is the "firstfruit" of a man's earnings or wealth, which always belongs to Him (Exod. 34:26). "Honor the Lord with thy substance," is a command, not an invitation. People who do not tithe are living off the blessings of the church but repudiating its claims through their actions. Non-tithers are similar to nonvoters, they are both irresponsible. The church is not a beggar pleading with people to part with their money, nor are ministers mendicants begging alms.

The prophet Malachi in his thunderings demanded, "Will a man rob God?" (Mal. 3:8). God indicted Israel for robbing Him of tithes and offerings. Now, how can you rob someone of what is not theirs?

The tithe is the Lord's (Lev. 27:30). Since the tithe is God's and not ours, if we do not give the tithe we rob God. If the tithe is the Lord's, which it is, and we give it, then we really have not given anything of our own until we give above the tithe.

When we give, especially when we give beyond our tithes, we enter into true sowing and reaping. When you tithe, God promises to save you from disasters the devourer would plan for you (Mal. 3:11). But when you give offerings, something will be "given to you: good measure, pressed down, shaken together, and running over" (Luke 6:38), whether tangible or intangible. Tangible gifts can have incredibly rich intangible returns.

Ruben is a great example. Ruben and his wife attended a "Sweetheart Meeting" where, at the end of the meeting, I asked couples who desired help in their marriages to come forward for prayer. I didn't know him and his wife, but something about them standing before me caught my attention.

"When was the last time you took your wife on a honeymoon?" I asked Ruben.

Ruben answered truthfully, "I have never taken my wife on a honeymoon."

Ruben remembers that "at this point you graciously blessed us with the money in your pocket so we could go on our first honeymoon." I had spontaneously reached in my pocket and handed them $220, all my travel expense allowance.

What I didn't know until Ruben wrote me weeks later was that they had never gone on a honeymoon because they were never married! Living together for seven years, having become Christians just nine months before the meeting that night, they stopped having sex two months earlier until they could save enough to be married.

Ruben wrote, "With eight children between us, saving money was hard, especially since I was unemployed and a recovering drug addict. When I was saved and delivered from drugs, I chose to depend on my Lord for everything we did. We had been praying earnestly for the money to get married when we went to the meeting."

They were married three days later, on Valentine's Day. The money he received that night covered the license and three nights at a nice hotel. But Ruben explains the amazing part of the story this way:

"We came to your meeting with enough money to cover our gas and parking. Well, as you were taking the offering I remembered I had $2.20. The Holy Spirit spoke to me and said, 'Who is your Provider, who do you trust?' Needless to say, I put my $2.20 in the offering . . . and then we were blessed with the miracle. What an awesome move of God!"

The principle Ruben's obedience illustrates is: *You gain by giving what you cannot buy with money.*

The intangible results Ruben found far outweighed any value of the tangible gift. Ruben gave his last $2.20 and received a hundred times more in return, plus a new marriage, edified children, respect as a man, increased faith in God, and a measure of manhood he never had before.

Men who give gain when God causes contracts to come their way, employers to decide in their favor, children to find a godly hero—an unlimited range of intangible blessings God generously gives, in ad-

dition to tangible financial returns. In return, out of a heart of gratitude, blessed men continue to give generously to God's work on
earth. The process started with God giving His best, Jesus Christ; it
continues when man surrenders his life in commitment to the Lord;
and is visibly expressed in tithes and offerings.

What a great statement of love and trust toward God, to give the
very means by which we live—money. Money, like sex, is an expression of love, made for loving and giving, not lusting and getting.

Giving money follows the giving of self (2 Cor. 8:1–5). When Zac-
cheus became a believer in Jesus the evidence of his changed heart
was his desire to make restitution of what he had criminally and
fraudulently garnered. The condition of his heart was shown in the
use of his money (Luke 19:5–9). Restitution was not a word, but an
action.

In a later story, Cornelius the centurion qualified to become the
gateway of the gospel to the Gentiles, by his praying . . . and his
offerings (Acts 10:2–8). Later still, the letter to the church at Corinth
tells how those who willingly gave of their means to support the
Gospel had first given themselves to God (2 Cor. 8).

Jesus said, "Make friends for yourselves friends by unrighteous
mammon, that when you fail, they may receive you" (Luke 16:9).
What He meant was not to buy friendships, but to use your money to
make friends for eternity. By tithes, gifts, and contributions the gospel is preached, men become sons of God, and friends are made for
eternity.

Money is a means of doing great good. God never cursed a fig tree
because it bore so much fruit that some of it fell to the ground and
spoiled; He only cursed it when it bore no fruit (Mark 11:12–14).
When we obey Him in giving, great good and great fruit follow.

"To obey is better than sacrifice" (1 Sam. 15:22) is a biblical principle.

Jesus said, "He who has My commandments and keeps them, it is
he who loves Me. And he who loves Me will be loved by My Father,
and I will love him and manifest Myself to him" (John 14:21). The
principle given is that obedience is the evidence of love, and manifestation is based on obedience.

At a conference in Milwaukee during the recession of 1984, I intended to pray for men who were experiencing financial distress
from the downturn. During the time of ministry, I happened to ask

how many who were having difficulties had not been faithful in their tithes and offerings. Almost 100 percent admitted they had not been consistent.

At that moment I realized these men were trying to compensate by the sacrifice of prayer for what they had been losing through their disobedience in not being faithful in their contributions, tithes, and offerings. It can't be done. What was needed was a return to faithfully contributing to the gospel and trusting God for divine compensation.

God's abundance is without limit. God puts no limitation on faith and faith puts no limitation on God.[1]

Jesus memorialized the woman who expended her most priceless possession on Him stating, "Wherever this gospel is preached in the whole world, what this woman has done will also be told" (Matt. 26:13). What He did for her, He will do for you.

Chapter 18
Positive Stress

My house is in California, but our office is in Dallas. The staff arrives in Dallas at 7:00 A.M., 5:00 A.M. my time, so by 5:30 in the morning on any given day, I can have a crisis brewing and not even know it—unless I call in. Let me share one recent case with you.

After restlessly preparing for a Christian Men's Event through the night, I called the office in the morning only to find some confusion and disorganization. No sooner was that resolved than a crisis call came from a member of a board on which I serve. I was already under pressure that day to complete a chapter of this book, but had a minister from overseas coming to see me, and was undecided on how to divide my time. Then a friend called for counsel. Each of my children called in succession. Paul had a business problem; Lois, a deputy district attorney, was concerned about an upcoming murder trial; Joann was having difficulties with her sons. The pressure was on.

At midmorning I still had not gone to the beach for my normal morning prayer. When I finally made my way downstairs, I found Nancy sifting through a stack of prayer requests that I was sure represented every ill ever visited on mankind. The newspaper on the counter caught my eye as I opened the cupboard to pour myself a bowl of cereal, which I discovered we didn't have. It was the day after statewide elections, and from the looks of the headlines, we would have some grim years ahead of us in government. I growled something about the world falling apart and felt the air around me tingle with static electricity.

Calmly and sweetly Nancy looked up from the table and said with a smile, "A wise man once said, 'Pressure always magnifies.'"

Pressure does magnify things. She was right. I knew what the sequence of thought would be next: that the world was terrible, I was doing it no good, there was no reason for me to be alive; everyone around me was in deep distress, and I was worthless as a friend, father, minister, and counselor. If I let myself go, I would experience those fivefold temptations experienced by Elijah. Men under stress face these temptations that seem too much to bear: depression, despair, resignation, failure, and inferiority.

Nancy's comment caught me, though. Instantly deflated from my tension, I sank down on a kitchen chair and willingly let her minister to me. The conference would be great. The ministry was going well. The kids had each been through the same thing before and were very capable of overcoming all. The board meeting was in God's hands. My friend could wait until next week. The book would get written, and why don't we just let ourselves relax and enjoy this visiting minister for a few hours. What a relief!

Stress is normal to life. Change is normal to life, and stress is normal to change. Everywhere you look our world is in transition.

The forefathers settling America lived in times of stress. Fighting to be free from political tyranny, opening new frontiers in an ever-expanding country, working through tension with native Americans, using almost primitive transportation and equipment, were only some of the ingredients producing anxiety and distress. A major difference between then and now is the pace of life, distance between neighbors, and the moral quality of society.

In America today, it is reported that whites will be in a minority in just two decades. Forty percent of Southern California speaks Spanish. Reports indicate that more than 50 percent of downtown Los Angeles is owned by Japanese. Asians number in the top percentage of honor graduates from some American schools of higher education. Church leaders predict multiracial congregations will be the norm throughout the world. These statistics are neither positive nor negative in themselves, but just addressing and accepting the changes is stressful.

In things that are inherently negative, there are even more dramatic changes. In the U.S. there was a 618 percent increase in births out of wedlock over the last five years. The crime rate has increased 1,050 percent. More than $71 billion is lost annually through drugs, and $33,000 is stolen per addict per year. According to my insurance agent, the AIDS epidemic will make the bubonic plague of yesteryear look small. He believes like many others that insurance companies stand to lose hundreds of millions of dollars, and face bankruptcy and ruin, unless something is done.

Stress at almost intolerable levels is being experienced in every segment of life in every nation on earth. U.S. business is on the move, with a half million firms relocating to new facilities in 1989. Upheavals accompany such moves, with two-thirds of executives fired, demoted, or quitting.[1]

Now they say television isn't even relaxing. A recent study "found that the longer a person watched the set, the more drowsy, bored, sad, lonely and hostile he would become."[2] David Frost, the television personality, said, "Television is an invention that permits you to be entertained in your living room by people you wouldn't have in your home."[3]

Office stress follows many home. Recent reports say 28 percent of all managers bring stress home, but 57 percent say they rarely bring family tensions to work.[4] At the same time, studies indicate that stress in the home is often even greater than stress at work. Researchers say that women working outside the home are happier even though they experience greater stress from juggling home and work responsibilities.[5] The hypothesis is that paid employment is an antidote to depression in women, and work provides a sense of worth that they are not getting at home. Unemployment among men produced the highest levels of stress in every survey. Work problems and related financial difficulties are a central theme not only in male suicides, but also in suicide-homicide cases. Many men use work to avoid dealing with personal problems. Men work longer hours when they are facing problems, the idea being that if you keep busy, you don't have to feel. I'm not saying any of this is right or wrong, just that it's there.

New concerns for parents come from the insecurity and risk they feel leaving their children with child-care facilities. Finding someone responsible has become a high-risk, high-stress venture for single mothers especially.[6]

Children eat breakfast in the morning looking at other children's pictures on milk cartons who have disappeared, been kidnapped, or lost. Fingerprinting children is commonplace. Date-rape, murder, and violence on campuses has brought fear to students and barricades to dormitories. In inner cities, both the young and the aged fear to venture outside their houses because of gang violence on their streets. They are, in effect, being held hostage by rampaging youth.

Financial stress is universally felt. Debtor nations are at the mercy of others, while those who loan are beholden to prop up the failing economies of those who borrow.

Personal debt on the individual level kills the productivity through which nations became strong. Easy credit allures. High interest credit cards are proliferating among unemployed college students in America. College presidents are using their time to battle the crisis created by greed.

Some young married couples are encouraged by salesmen, marketers, advertisers, and bankers to have all they want through easy payment plans, only to be trapped by usury. Seduced by avarice, they try to accumulate in three years of marriage what it took their parents thirty years to obtain. Debt puts a strain on the relationship that often fractures it. Some recognize temptation for what it is and others don't.

There is a story about a man who went to his banker to get a loan. The banker told him he might get it and might not.

"Tell you what I'll do," the banker said. "I've got one good eye and one glass eye. Tell me which one is the glass eye and I'll give you the loan."

The man looked carefully and long into the banker's eyes and then said, "The right eye."

"How did you know?" asked the startled banker.

"Because I thought I saw a little mercy in that eye," the man answered.

Financial pressure, like any stress, can drive men to desperation, but needn't overwhelm the real man. As Nancy ministered to me and my peace returned that morning, I remembered a day earlier when my friend Jim had telephoned me to say, "In two more months I'll be completely out of debt."

"I'm thrilled for you," I replied. "How much did you owe?"

"Five million dollars," he said, "and now after two years I'm going to be debt free. It was a struggle but we made it."

Bankers had loaned him money to pay the interest on money he had borrowed, snowballing until his debt finally totalled five million dollars. A successful real estate developer, he now saw very little of his money. Almost all was going to banks. The pressure was intense. Then one night in prayer, he sought God's strategy through wisdom from the Word, and God dropped a gift of faith in his heart. As he believed by faith that God would see him through, he scribbled out new terms for handling the debt. The next day he put a halt to the cycle by telling the bankers he wasn't playing their game anymore, and laid down the new terms God had helped him formulate. The bankers fumed and fussed, but agreed. Now after only two years he was to be totally out of debt.

"You are a poor specimen if you can't stand the pressure of adversity" (Prov. 24:10 LB).

Jesus was without personal stress in Himself, though He bore the sins of the world. Admitting that He was only doing what he saw the Father do, relieved Him from the pressure of having to perform on His own. He had the backing of heaven for all He did (John 5:19–20). Regardless of the turmoil in the world around Him, He was without feelings of insecurity. Neither was He insecure in His identity. His open confession of Himself came from His established heart (John 10:30–42). Spoken with perfect equanimity, His testimony was attested by His deeds. "Believe me for what I say, or believe for my work's sake," He told people (John 14:12; 10:37–38).

He never manipulated, threatened, or gave ultimatums to those who heard Him. He spoke "as one having authority, and not as the scribes" (Matt. 7:29). This authority came in part from His knowledge of who He was, His purpose in life, and an identity with which He was in perfect agreement.

Real men are Christlike. Identified with Jesus, secure in that identity, acting in faith on God's Word, believing God will perform what He says, they move through life's trials and circumstances with confidence and face adversity with courage.

Pressure is normal and even needed in life. The right amount of tension in a guitar or piano string is necessary for fine tuning. Too much and it will snap. Water, steam, and ice are made from the same substance, as are carbon, graphite, and diamonds. It's the pressure that makes the difference. The more pressure matter is able to withstand, the more valuable it becomes. It's the same with people.

I'll never forget what I learned from a pastor friend in Florida who was undergoing pressure that seemed unbearable. A godly man, desiring to do the right thing in the midst of much wrong, he had to struggle to maintain his personal equilibrium, to minister in love and grace, and to determine the will of God for his life and congregation.

During that time he found some positive aspects of stress in his life. When he taught them I never forgot them, and pass them on to you.

- Stress is necessary for spiritual growth (James 1:2–4).
- Stress produces more love in committed people (Rom. 5:3–5).
- Stress produces a greater degree of sanctification (1 Peter 4:1).
- Testing prepares you for greater works (Rev. 3:12).
- Stress causes the greatest need for prayer (Phil. 4:6).
- Stress comes from resisting Satan (1 Peter 5:9).
- Testing comes before victory (James 1:12; Rom. 8:35–37).
- Stress produces seeking after God, and that glorifies Him (1 Peter 4:12–13).

Stress is not a new phenomenon in life. Everyone in every generation has faced their own peculiar pressures. Leadership always has it. The greater the responsibility, the greater the pressure.

Elijah was a "man with a nature like ours" (James 5:17). He faced his own time of pressure, stress, and the fivefold temptations that are common to man. Stressed from contests, threats, and physical depletion, he sat under a tree and asked to die (1 Kings 19:4).

Elijah was no longer on Mt. Carmel listening to the cheers of the crowd as he challenged and defeated the prophets of Baal. Gone was the glory of the day, the fire of God's presence, and the revelation of God's power. Behind him was the elation of winning against all odds. Yesterday's victories were now only memories. He was facing his greatest battle—alone—not against false prophets, but against his own personal temptations.

He wanted to die.

Elijah was to learn what another prophet would write centuries later, that God will not deny His people in their weakness. "Even when we are too weak to have any faith left, [God] remains faithful to us and will help us, for he cannot disown us who are part of himself, and he will always carry out his promises" (2 Tim. 2:13 LB).

If we are in Christ, and Christ is in us, then God cannot deny us in our time of trouble or temptation. If He did He would be denying Himself, and that He will not do.

Our personal feelings, sentiments, attitudes, or emotions do not annul the promises of God. Elijah was depleted physically, depressed mentally, despairing spiritually, and his will to fight was gone.

But God traded his strength for Elijah's weakness. Elijah rebounded, completed his ministry, and was ushered into heaven in front of Elisha who saw a chariot of fire take him (2 Kings 2:11).

Elijah traded his juniper tree for a chariot of fire.[7]

But God was the phrase that changed Joseph's life centuries earlier (Gen. 50:20). Sold down the river, falsely accused and jailed, Joseph never lost faith in God. God eventually elevated him to the highest position in government. What men meant for evil, God meant for good in Joseph's life.

All trials and temptations will end positively if committed to God. God always starts on the positive and ends on the positive. It is the nature of God to change things in our lives for the good. There is pressure in change, but change is the only constant in maturity.

All that is stressful in your life today has the potential for good or for harm. Determine to be changed through the refining fire of pressure, believe God to enable you to overcome the fivefold temptations, lose yourself in identity with Jesus Christ, seek His wisdom in the particularly critical decisions, and let stress work for the good to make you a stronger man.

Chapter 19
Peace for All Seasons

The frigate gently rolled, barely visible on the ocean, with the early morning clouds just lifting over its stacks. From the deck, my shipmates and I could see the destroyers and cruisers we supported looming large in the distance. With the lifting fog, we could make out tiny moving specks which were the Navy crewmen on deck.

Suddenly, Japanese bombers screamed through the clearing sky and began to drop their payloads. The sailors swung into action, bombarding the air with rounds of ammunition. The bombers circled and returned. Out of their ranks came the kamikaze attackers, diving headlong to sink our ships by suicidally destroying their planes.

I stood awestruck, stunned, on the deck of the frigate. My shipmates and I had been at sea for an entire year doing convoy and escort duty without ever touching land, but this was the fiercest and closest action we'd seen. We only had a three-inch and some 40mm and 20mm guns with which to defend ourselves, and all guns were firing.

We watched spellbound as the battle unfolded. The smell of burning oil, exploding ammunition, and stench from the beach putrefied the salty air. The sounds of screaming planes, booming guns, and exploding bombs overpowered our ears until all we could hear were rumbling noises. I looked up after a few minutes, which felt like hours, and saw a Japanese plane heading straight for our deck.

If I had been stunned before, now I was frozen. I had not lived for God in years, but I called on Him like He was my best friend. I promised I'd serve Him if He got me out this. I stared in disbelief at what was surely to be the last thing I would see on this earth.

Suddenly, the kamikaze plane dove into the ocean, just missing us, and exploded. Through the smoke, I could barely see the pieces floating on the water. It was gone. Vanished. My attention fell back to the ships but the battle was ending.

The calm of the ocean returned. The men on the destroyers started cleaning up, taking care of the wounded, putting out fires, beginning the rebuilding process to prepare for the next battle.

Months later when I was finally home, peace was eminent. I knew I wouldn't be back at sea again because the war was ending. When I went home to discuss my plans with my mother, she asked me about the battle I had experienced. It was etched in my mind, and I'd had months to relive it. I told her about it in vivid detail. When I described the kamikaze plane exploding, she shrieked, "That was it!"

She had been lying in bed that same day when suddenly she sat upright and cried, "My son!" She didn't know what awakened her, but she prayed fervently, beseeching God's protection in my behalf, interceding with Him to rescue me, believing for a miracle. God heard my mother's prayers.

There are two things I learned in that war. One is the power of prayer. The other is that peace is worth fighting for. Peace comes from victory.

In 1988 I was in England when Mr. Reagan and Mr. Gorbachev signed their historic treaty. One of England's cynical newspapers ran a picture of Mr. Chamberlain and Adolph Hitler signing the old, broken treaty at Munich before World War II. Mr. Chamberlain was deceived into believing Hitler's promise of peace because he wanted so desperately to avoid war. Britain's paper ran the Reagan-Gorbachev story with the headline, "Western Munich." They sarcastically showed their disbelief of any negotiated peace treaty signed by a communist leader. They had good reason. Dimitry Manuilski, an instructor at the Lenin School of Political Warfare in Moscow, wrote in 1930 about communism's plan to defeat the free world. "We shall begin by launching the most spectacular peace movement on record," he wrote. "There shall be electrifying overtures and unheard-of concessions. As soon as their guard is down, we will smash them with our clenched fist."[1]

During the Reagan-Gorbachev summit, twenty-five wars raged in various parts of the world. Of them, only one was between nations. The others were fought within countries, faction against faction, brother against brother. A research institute provided these shocking statistics: "Overall, since the end of World War II in 1945, the death total in wars, rebellions and uprisings of various sorts have taken the lives of 17 million people."[2]

According to the Bible, peace will not come through treaties, summit conferences, or negotiated settlements as long as men have war in their hearts. The state of the heart is at fault, not just the politics involved.

David, king of Israel, had a trusted friend and advisor named Ahithophel (2 Sam. 15), who possessed great wisdom and stood as a spokesman for God. David relied on him. When David's son, Absalom, tried to steal the kingdom from his father, Ahithophel defected to serve Absalom (2 Sam. 15:12). Knowing that Ahithophel's advice to Absalom could defeat him, David sent another trusted counselor to confound the wisdom of Ahithophel. The counselor posed as a defector also, and convinced Absalom to undermine the advice of Ahithophel. David's strategy succeeded. Absalom was defeated and killed, and Ahithophel committed suicide (2 Sam. 17:23).

David was heartbroken at what happened. He not only mourned his son, but also lamented the loss of his friend, and grieved over the betrayal. David wrote,

> For it is not an enemy who reproaches me;
> Then I could bear it.
> Nor is it one who hates me who has magnified himself
> against me;
> Then I could hide myself from him.
> But it was you, a man my equal,
> My companion and my acquaintance.
> We took sweet counsel together,
> And walked to the house of God in the throng.
> (Ps. 55:12–14)

Later he said of Ahithophel,

> The words of his mouth were smoother than butter,
> But war was in his heart;
> His words were softer than oil,
> Yet they were drawn swords. (Ps. 55:21)

David learned the lesson: There is no peace with men who have war in their hearts.

The angels knew this when they pronounced Christ's birth saying, "On earth peace, good will toward men" (Luke 2:14). The correct translation is peace "among men" not "toward men." Peace can only be found in the hearts of men whose hearts are filled with the good will of God, with His love shed abroad in them, and filled with concern for the well-being of others. It is perhaps self-evident, but men with war in their hearts will never be men of peace.

Whether it is in marriage, business, civic enterprise, religion, social intercourse, there is no peace where war is in the heart.

Peace comes from the heart, not the peace table.

Generally there is only real peace after total victory, and little or none from a negotiated compromise. America found that true through two different wars. World War II was a "soldiers' war." Noted military leaders such as Eisenhower, MacArthur, Bradley, Patton, Nimitz, and Marshall led men into battle to win a victory. Our enemies were defeated in that war, and they eventually relegated themselves to peaceful pursuits. The victors reveled in it. The Allied Forces went home in glory and honor, lauded and decorated.

Vietnam, on the other hand, was a "politicians' war." Major decisions were made by committee through compromise. Soldiers resisted the politicians' tactics and argued for more battlefield efficiency, but ultimately "political expediency" prevailed. America's policy makers finally settled for a "truce." When the troops came home, a different homecoming awaited them. They came home in disgrace, suffered reproach, were looked at with disdain, and even spat upon. To this day some have suffered, not only from the war, but also from the rejection experienced on arriving back on native soil.

The soldiers were fighting for victory. The politicians were negotiating for compromise. Without victory, people wanted someone to blame. The soldiers bore the brunt of it. I've had men's meetings where Vietnam veterans stood just so the rest of us could cheer them and say, "Thank you!" They fought for us and for our country. They deserve our appreciation. God bless them.

Victory requires decisiveness in leaders, ruthlessness in discipline, and willingness to fight until the battle is over and the victory is won.

On the way to Calvary, Satan tempted Jesus to accept the recompense of reward without paying the price (Luke 4). This devilish temptation to compromise was an opportunity to avoid the ignominy of the Cross, with all it's the humiliation, shame, and agony. Jesus refused. He knew: *No cross, no crown!*

The Cross became the place of defeat for Satan, and victory for Jesus and all who would trust Him. Having defeated Satan, obtained the peace of His victory, Jesus can now offer those who believe and receive Him His peace, "Peace I leave with you, My peace I give to you; not as the world gives do I give to you" is His promise (John 14:27).

The peace this world offers is ephemeral, transitory, and without eternal substance, rooted in a nature that is at enmity with God; thus peace in the world can never come from this source.

Peace that Christ gives is the grounds for the security, safety, prosperity, and happiness for all men everywhere. It is issued in the spirit and its moral effect is not just an absence from guilt, but a clear conscience, quiet rest for the soul, an internal harmony in the spirit, and a beneficent relationship with fellow human beings. There is a rest of the spirit in the trust in Christ.

Varied are the causes of war in men's hearts:

The flesh lusts against the spirit (Gal. 5:17). Lusts war in the members (James 4:1).

Time constraints overwhelm us. Men who compromise with time are "lazy"; men who conquer time are "productive."

Convictions defect to convenience. Men who live by conviction are "strong"; men who live by convenience are "weak."

A man wrote from Tulsa after hearing me speak on this subject in a men's meeting. He had wrestled with pornography and lust throughout his life, from his early teens to his present thirties. No amount of Christian counsel or prayer seemed to help. One Friday, as he planned his indulgences while his wife was away for the weekend, he suddenly remembered the words of that meeting: "I will not compromise."

"I fell flat on my face and cried out to God, confessing my sins," he wrote. "The words *I will not compromise* kept running through my mind. I took index cards and wrote it on them. I put them on the mirror where I shave, the refrigerator, the dashboard of my car. With the continual help of God and the prayers of others, those four words became a reality in my life."

The presence of God cannot be separated from the power of God.

To the degree men yield to temptations, there is a loss of both peace and power (Rom. 8:6). The devil's playground is the defeated soul. What is yielded to grows stronger, while what is resisted grows weaker (Rom. 6:16).

No wonder there is such power, liberty, peace, and joy in the Cross! Jesus Christ said, "My yoke is easy and My burden is light" (Matt. 11:30). Men yoked to lies, fraud, addictions, thievery, vanity, or arrogance carry a heavy burden. Men yoked to truth, honesty, love, repentance, and faith carry burdens that are light. Contrast the burdens and only a fool would not exchange bondage for liberty.

Fighting for victory is difficult, but the difficulty of the fight is far easier than bearing the consequences brought on by truce-making with besetting sins. One of the properties of discipline in the life of Jesus Christ was His ruthlessness. "If your eye causes you to sin, pluck it out!" He said. "If your hand or foot causes you to sin, cut it off and cast it from you" (Matt. 18:8–9). Jesus Christ had a ruthless attitude toward sin, and manifested it in His dedication to eradicate it. Men who would be Christlike cannot afford to play "footsie" with Satan or sin. Ruthlessness with self is necessary to excise both from life.

"A righteous man who falters before the wicked / Is like a murky spring and a polluted well" (Prov. 25:26). Joshua learned well the misery accompanying compromise after he succeeded Moses as leader of Israel. God's "scorched earth" policy was to keep Israel from subscribing to foreign gods. God told Joshua to defeat totally every nation in the land which He would give them. God, in turn, would make the Israelites conquerors wherever they fought. In Israel's triumphant march into Canaan, all the nations around them cringed in terror. The Gibeonites were a nation who feared Israel. They did not want to go up against Israel in battle, so they devised a scheme to deceive Joshua into making a truce with them. Wearing ragged clothes and carrying moldy bread, they met Joshua and claimed they came from a distant land, when in reality they lived in Canaan. Joshua fell for their ruse. He offered them fresh provisions and exchanged a peace treaty with them. When Joshua discovered their duplicity, it was too late. Joshua could not violate the treaty and had to surrender that part of the "Promised Land." As a result, the Gibeonites became a snare to the entire nation of Israel (Josh. 9).

Much of the misery of life can generally be traced to a truce with sin.

Agreement is one means of obtaining peace. I have taught for years that "the place of agreement is the place of power." The opposite also holds true, "the place of disagreement is the place of powerlessness."

This truth is valid on the personal and national level. Until the Gulf War, America suffered from the chasm that developed in the nation during Vietnam. In World War II the nation was united. In Vietnam it was divided. The Bible teaches, "Every kingdom divided against itself is brought to desolation, and a house divided against a house falls" (Luke 11:17). Disunity killed America's initiative during Vietnam, and the schism tended to a settlement by compromise and truce was the result—not victory. A truce in war is like a tie in football—nobody wins.

On the other hand, unity will generate power to any person or group of people. When America underwent another crisis called "Watergate," the country reeled under the weight of shame, slander, scandal, accusations, and a breakdown of trust. I remember one of those deeply involved testifying on TV, "We didn't start out as criminals. We were just men who compromised our convictions, and one thing led to another."

One thing held the nation together: the Constitution of the United States. The country was in agreement that the Constitution must be upheld. Agreement upon the written word saved the nation.

In the same way, agreement with the Word of God will save a man from compromise and make for peace. "Unite my heart to fear Your name," was the cry of the psalmist (Ps. 86:11). Scripture exhorts to "pursue the things that make for peace" (Rom. 14:19), and an established heart united in one purpose makes for peace.

In the tensions developed in a man's life between the choices of family and profession, recreation and work, ethics and cheating, church and pleasure, when the power of choice is exercised by obedience to God's Word, there is peace—harmony with God, self, and others. We wrestle between forces—godly, devilish, and fleshly—constantly. Submission to the godly will bring resistance to the devilish and power over the flesh.

The apostle Paul said, "All things are lawful for me, but I will not be brought under the power of any" (1 Cor. 6:12). He also said, "Do you not know that to whom you present yourselves slaves to obey, you are that one's slaves whom you obey, whether of sin to death, or of obedience to righteousness?" (Rom. 6:16).

Everything in life is under our power of choice, but once the choice is made, we become the servant to the choice.

The choice of drug use makes a slave of substance abusers; dropping out of school produces poverty, paupers indentured to ignorance and the limitations it brings; our choice of a marriage partner can make marriage become a rich, rewarding life or a poor existence. Selecting the right food and opting for exercise will serve the body well so it can be worn in good health. Enjoying the disciplines of study and developing the powers of concentration serve knowledge which translates into authority. Submission to patience is the key to finding the right woman.

Choices determine destiny.

Abraham made a wrong decision, and the entire world was affected. Childless at the age of eighty-six, he went along with Sarah's advice to have a child with her maid, Hagar. He impregnated Hagar, and she bore Ishmael. Realizing his error, Abraham decided to do right and trust God for Sarah to conceive a child. God was faithful and gave them Isaac, the child of promise (Gen. 15, 18). But the result of Abraham's defection from faith, making a decision after the flesh and not the spirit, is the enmity between the descendants of Sarah and Hagar—the Jews and the Arabs (Gen. 16:11–12).

Once you choose, you become the servant of that choice. A public school administrator in Maryland heard this statement in one of our videos and used it as personal motivation. Over the years, he had gradually gained about seventy pounds. He looked at a sandwich and chips the day after seeing the video and said, "Sandwich and chips, if I eat you, I'm going to be a slave to you!" He enrolled in a weight-loss program that very week, lost the weight, has kept it off for two years, and enjoys peace of heart and mind. Making the right choice led to peace.

There are many different facets of peace.

- The Bible says, "Peace is the umpire for knowing the will of God" (Col. 3:15 AB).
- There is a "rest" that comes from God (Heb. 4:9). It overcomes anxiety.

- There is a contentment that God gives (1 Tim. 6:6). It overcomes restlessness.
- There is a sense of having found something with God (Luke 17:21). It overcomes searching.
- There is a sense of peace and security with God (John 14:27; Phil. 4:7; Ps. 119:165). It overcomes strife.

God is not the author of confusion (1 Cor. 14:33). He has made provision for peace through Christ. Jesus is called the "Prince of Peace" (Isa. 9:6). He promises to give us peace (John 14:27).

His message is a word of peace (Eph. 2:14–17). A word of wisdom from the Holy Spirit brought peace to the early Church when they were at an impasse (Acts 15).

Jesus held His peace (Matt. 26:63). Men lose their peace by opening their mouths when they should keep them shut. A raging fire is made from a little kindling, and one word spoken at the wrong time can start an argument that ends in tragedy.

The truest, fullest peace comes through Christ, knowing that He fought and won the peace. It is a wonderful thing to know that by His indwelling Spirit in us, He will bring forth His victory and peace in our lives.

Jesus looked over Jerusalem and wept because they did not recognize the hour of their visitation from God. He exclaimed, "Would that you had known personally, even at least in this your day, the things that make for peace," for freedom from all the distresses that are experienced as the result of sin and upon which your peace, that is, your security, safety, prosperity and happiness depends (Luke 19:42 AB).

Don't make their mistake and not recognize the hour of your visitation from God. Achieve peace through Christ, and have this quality of life in which the real man enjoys a full sense of security and safety, and prosperity and happiness flourish.

Chapter 20
Leadership That Works

Leaders are made, not born.

Men were born with an "ego mastery" to equip them for leadership. Through creation the capabilities of leadership are inherent in the nature of every man. Every man to some extent is a leader, either for good or evil.

Three characteristics are distinguished in popular leaders, but God lists six qualifications for leadership in His Church.

The three distinguishing characteristics of popular leaders who command a following are: uninhibited in life-style, fervent in spirit, and zealous of good works.

Uninhibited in life-style represents identifying with purposes and goals in life without thought to self. Fervent in spirit is likened to the contagion in disease that is only found when the fever is present. Zealous is the ardent, impassioned, and persevering desire of a cause or purposeful pursuit in life. Any one is enough to command a following; any two can make a musician a star or create a political movement from a simple boycott; all three found in one man can change the course of history.

Winston Churchill, a stouthearted leader during World War II, rallied his nation through his influence gained by his ability to communicate. His speeches are still studied as models for students who desire to lead. Mr. Churchill is said to have possessed nerve and verve, chilling determination, words of resolve (positive and potent), certitude of rightness in his moral-compass heading, and implacable courage. Uninhibited in life-style, fervent in spirit, and zealous for his cause, he commanded a following not only in his own nation but others as well, and helped bring defeat to Adolph Hitler's mad designs for this world.

Jesus Christ is the epitome of these characteristics, the source of their origination, and the ultimate expression of them in ministry. He was uninhibited in his life-style in that He was totally identified with the Father (John 10:30). His fervency was exhibited in His diligent application to the Father's will (John 5:30, 6:38). And His zeal for the Father's house was evident not only when He drove the money-changers out of the temple (Mark 11:15–17), but in the surrender of His life. Men followed Him, devoted themselves to Him, and gave themselves over to His cause. Real men still do.

Christ fulfilled not just these three dynamic characteristics, but the six qualifications God requires for true leadership.

In his letter to Timothy, Paul, under the influence of the Holy Spirit, listed a catalog for church bishops that is applicable to men in leadership anywhere today. A leader is to be blameless (above reproach), the husband of one wife, temperate, sober-minded, of good behavior, hospitable, able to teach, not given to wine, not violent, not greedy for money, gentle, not quarrelsome, not covetous, one who rules his own house well, having his children in submission with all reverence, not a novice, and of good reputation (1 Tim. 3).

In cataloging these qualifications, they fall naturally under the headings of reputation, ethics, morality, temperament, habits, and maturity.

REPUTATION

A man's reputation is seen in the regard given his name. "A good name is to be chosen rather than great riches" (Prov. 22:1). A man's reputation is established by the esteem in which he is held, the respect shown and honor given.

Real men recognize the importance of their reputation among peers, and also value their reputation with their wife and children.

One of my heroes is a man in New Orleans who stopped everything he was doing, and then changed his entire life for the sake of his family. It began when his sons were arrested for a second time, and it was at that time when he determined to find out what was going on. When he questioned them, he found out that his good reputation among peers, employees, his church, and others was not shared by his own sons. Others thought he was energetic about the Lord's business, successful in personal and media ministry, and held him in high regard; but his sons thought he was more interested in things other than them, that he was willing to sacrifice them on the altar of his fame, and they resented Jesus for taking all their dad's time and energy.

Shocked and startled, he realized he needed to do something to repair the damage done by his zealousness. Moses in his zeal killed an Egyptian. This man in his zeal was destroying his relationship with his sons. He took a leave of absence from work and spent time with his family, lavishing his attention on his sons, praying over every detail in their lives. Months later he stood before a group of men and told of the wonderful new relationship he had with his family. He had finally gained a good reputation with his children.

This man understood the necessity of qualifying for his leadership position. He valued his stature with his family more than the regard he had from his peers.

ETHICS

Ethics is more than a study for college professors who major in philosophy. It's a major guideline to relationships, whether in business, marriage, or crime. A study reported that the new generation, ages thirteen to twenty-nine, has little or no understanding of ethics, and little or no desire to study or be guided by ethics. They consider ethics to be archaic posturing without merit for modern men. Perhaps this is due to the lack of ethics in home life. Sibling rivalry is common when parental ethics are violated by showing favoritism among the children. Ethical behavior by parents in regard to children is necessary to balanced relationships.

In business and government, however, the study of ethics is booming. It is the new cry of responsible adults. Those involved have found even criminals have a code of what they consider to be ethical conduct that is to be adhered to. If someone violates it, he is expendable. What has made ethics so "hot" are things like the case of Mr. Milken and his culpability in insider trading on Wall Street. His lawyers pleaded for leniency based on the good he had done for society, and asked the court to ignore the near total wreckage of businesses, the loss of billions of dollars, and the heavy burden the taxpaying citizens will have to bear for years.

A lack of ethics blinds men to their own wrongdoing. The total lack of ethics in governments of many nations is the root cause of the chaos and destruction of nations and peoples. National ethics in America can be traced in its roots to the application of biblical principles. Where moral absolutes are missing in individuals, families, or nations, there is no foundation for ethical behavior.

Immoral but religious ethics are represented in the New Testament by the Pharisees and Sadducees. Pharisees were the legalists who took things that were relative and made them absolutes; and Sadducees were those who took absolutes and made them relative. There are still secular and sacred pharisees today doing the same thing.

MORALITY

Morality is a a system of ethical conduct. Morality relates to principles of right and wrong behavior, and can be called "virtue." *Virtue* in one sense is used in the Bible synonymously with *courage*.

Moral cowardice is the bane of manhood, moral courage its virtue.

Morality is more than "yes" and "no," good and bad. There is an immorality to wasting life, failing to do right, making poor decisions, that goes beyond the morality we fight for in keeping ourselves pure from lust, compromise, and more common moral issues.

Mike Singletary, the great all-pro football linebacker with the Chicago Bears, invited me to his hometown one evening to speak to some of his friends and teammates. Upon arrival I found he had rented a hotel auditorium and invited a great number of people for the evening. I was, and am, deeply impressed by his moral courage and the importance he placed on ministering to those around him.

He stood up in front of them and said, "Here's a guy who I think has something to say: my friend, Ed Cole," and sat down, as eloquent an introduction as was needed. I talked to his friends about the same five reasons for courage I have written and lectured about around the world. We need courage to: face reality, admit need, confess wrong, change; make decisions, and hold convictions.

Many men will exhibit courage on the football field or in their professions, but balk at exhibiting moral courage in the locker room among the profane, at home in making decisions, or in attending church on the weekend. As a result they become cowardly toward Christ.

Men often fail to qualify for leadership because of moral cowardice. Moral cowardice also leads some to relinquish the leadership they do have because of intimidation by others. Hal used to feel intimidated by other men. Hal was responsible for leading a large group of men in his city and had to deal with men of renown, wealth, power, and prestige. Never having had the kind of success these men enjoyed, Hal's feelings of inferiority were beginning to trouble him and cause him to doubt his place of leadership. His pastor and I,* together with him, sought a private place for prayer. As his pastor prayed, I heard him say something that was incomparable in wisdom, and became a healing word for Hal.

"Lord, teach Hal that he does not have to be a peer with men he is called to serve," was the pastor's word of wisdom. It immediately relieved Hal of all insecurity and inferiority around other men, and has given him confidence in leadership.

I heard in his prayer wisdom that is the solution for pastors who have been called to serve successful, prominent men in their congregations. Others, such as Hal, are often intimidated by successful men, unable to meet their needs because of a sense of inferiority. So they settle for mediocrity. We often look for morality in the way of temperance and sexual purity in our Christian leaders, but God looks for even more. Moral courage qualifies men to be leaders of those they esteem to be greater than themselves.

During a visit to the U.S. Naval Academy, Secretary of the Navy James H. Webb, Jr., addressed the men and women of the Brigade of Midshipmen, and in defining true leaders said,

> A true leader must set the example. You cannot ask of your subordinates that which you do not demand of yourself. The best leaders make decisions, have a clear sense of mission, and express it. They have the courage to do what is right and to make sure that those who are under their authority do the same. Courage, both moral and physical, is a character trait that can infect others.[1]

TEMPERAMENT

Richard told me about the time he was selling his businesses to a large, powerful company. In discussing the sale and its terms, the New York lawyers attempted to intimidate Richard, his dad, his partner, and their hometown lawyers. Imposing, manipulating, and exploiting, the big-time lawyers tried everything to wring concessions out of them, take all they could, and leave them with as little as possible.

To stay on top of them, Richard consciously refused to be badgered, goaded into anger, or cowed into subservience. He depended on the temperament God had given him through years of renewing his mind with the Word of God and becoming a new creature in heart, soul, and emotions.

"I finally just told them they needed me more than I needed them," Richard said. "I gave them my terms, take it or leave it. We went through a year of negotiations before it was all done—but in the end I won."

Richard's boldness and firmness in negotiations had their roots in his personal beliefs, and were based on knowing who he was in God, and that being right didn't mean he had to be bullied or beaten by anybody. Men who browbeat mock those beaten. Richard was neither.

A temperate man doesn't make decisions based on the emotion of the moment or the personal gratification he can garner, but on the merits of the decision itself. The real man's criteria for decision making are: Is it biblical, moral, ethical, legal? Holding to that standard, refusing to be swayed otherwise, keeping personal feelings in hand help determine good leadership.

HABITS

Physical habits find their root in mental traits. How a man thinks, what his secret thought patterns may be, is basic to behavior. Remember, actions follow beliefs and emotions follow actions.

Change a mind, change a habit, change a life.

When Israel entered the Promised Land the people were told to destroy the idols and images of the nations that occupied the land so that idolatry would not become a snare to them. Their leaders led them in tearing down the great idols in the cities, but winked at the "high places" of the land and allowed the people to worship at them (2 Chron. 15:16–17). The "high places" represented places they retreated to in secrecy to worship false gods. Eventually the high places led to the official reinstitution of idolatry.

The "high places" in men's minds are those secret thoughts:

strongholds of nostalgia, sentiment, and fantasy into which men can retreat on occasion to satisfy their natural desire. Creative mental habit patterns are constructive, but indulging in compulsions and obsessions is destructive. Fantasizing in lust through pornography seems at first to be a nonhazardous occupation—merely going up to some "high place" for a few moments of recreational worship to an image created in the mind. It eventually finds its release and can lead to incest, rape, homosexuality, and deadly diseases.

God's "scorched earth policy" regarding idolatry is to tear down idols, "high places" and all.

Sons who are unwilling to forgive their fathers their sins, who hold grudges against them, actually find pleasure in thinking of ways to hurt their dads. "High place" imaginations that worship the idols of hatred and vengeance hold sway over such worshipers.

Such habits of the mind are practices that should not be tolerated in any man's life. They can lead to despicable actions.

Habitually washing the mind with the water of the Word of God (Eph. 5:26), practicing positive prayers, repetitively quoting Scripture, methodically and systematically reading the Bible, routinely worshiping, all develop godly traits, build character, and give quality to life.

We are creatures of habit. Habits can be developed by default or determination. It has been my privilege in the past to work with some great men, but perhaps the greatest of all I had known (who, because of humility, won't permit me to use his name) arrived at his stature as a world leader by choosing to read at least one great book every week of his life. Over the last thirty years he has read more than two thousand of the greatest books ever written. And people wonder why he is where he is? Books, not dogs, are a man's best friend.

MATURITY

The marks of a mature man can be seen in a variety of ways: the facets of character, friends he chooses, decisions he makes, responsibility he accepts, leadership he exercises, and so on.

Leaders are men who determine to influence, while followers only happen to influence.

Leaders are those who: set the example, are decisive, have a clear sense of mission, show courage, accept accountability, understand true loyalty, get the job done, take care of their people, are able to motivate others, are able to communicate properly, and are content to be themselves.

In 1987, in Harare, Zimbabwe, three ladies gave me what they called "a word from God." An ex-police chief inspector was helping to coordinate our men's meetings in that country and brought me a message one afternoon that these women believed I needed to hear the word. Tight scheduling prevented me from meeting with them so he became the mediator to give me their message. Being a former military officer, he first gave me a background briefing on his country. Rhodesia was at war for fourteen years until it became Zimbabwe. During the war, the men spent six weeks in the bush fighting, then six weeks at home working before returning to the bush again to fight. The tension and anxiety in the home and nation was incredible.

Godly women in the churches of the country began to engage in intercessory prayer for their men and nation. As time went by, they began to see themselves as "Esthers." The Bible records Esther as a queen who interceded for her people and nation before her husband the king. An edict was given to annihilate her race of people in the King's country. When her uncle discovered the terrible plot, he exhorted her to boldness in interceding for her people, saying, "Who knows whether you have come to the kingdom for such a time as this" (Esther 4:14). Rhodesian women, praying for their nation, began to believe they had come to their nation for such a time as this civil war.

Then the war ended. Rhodesia became Zimbabwe. The men came home. But now something new required their attention and intercession as much as before. The men in their eyes had become passive, complacent, and lethargic. "Esthers" saw the need for intercession as much now in peacetime as during wartime.

For seven more years they continued in uninterrupted intercession. One day, while in prayer, these ladies were impressed with something they believed was a "word" for the men of their nation. They held onto it, laying it up "for an appointed time" (Hab. 2:3). A year later they heard the teaching that "manhood and Christlikeness are synonymous," which we brought to their city. They believed the "word" they had was for me and the Christian Men's Network.

It was so simple at first I almost dismissed it, but over a period of time it grew in my spirit until today I believe it is truly a word for men not only of Zimbabwe, but of this entire generation—men who have let the women take the leadership role in the church, home, and nation.

The word they gave was: "There was a time for Esthers, but today is a time for Daniels."

Powerful!

These were women who had to bear the burden in the heat of the day, bear the responsibilities men dropped when they vacated their places of leadership, and remained absent from them when returning home. They saw it as pertaining to their nation; I saw it as pertaining to men the world over.

Now is the time for men to accept the spiritual and moral leadership of the home, church, and community. This is a call from God, not just women, for men to be like Daniels in this present world, leaders in home, church, and country.

Today is a day for Daniels. God speaks to you to cast down the "high places" and become concerned about the six characteristics that qualify you to be His leader. First and foremost every real man establishes his relationship to God. With that relationship the real man approaches every day, conscientiously living out the characteristics that qualify him to become a leader—the leader God created him to be.

Part 6

Real Roles

■ ■ ■

Chapter 21

The Irresistible Husband

From the Bayou country of Louisiana comes a story of Cajun humor that carries a point we can apply to marriage.

"Wha's dat unna yo shirt?" the friend asks.

"It's the dyn-o-mite ah've strapped to mah chest," replies the man.

"Why you got dyn-o-mite tied ta yo chest?" the friend inquires.

"You know how Louis always come up to me and poke me inna chest all the time? Well, dah next time he poke me inna chest, I gonna blow his han' off!"

Trying to remedy an annoying situation was going to cause him more harm than good. The same can happen in marriage. A husband may try to correct situations in his marriage without using wisdom or understanding, and thereby alienate himself further from his wife and family. This happens all too often.

Recently, on a television talk show, women vented their anger toward their mates and dates. In one thirty-minute segment, remarks such as these erupted: "All men are jerks;" "He was simply more boy than man;" "All men live by their primal passions." Tragically, these comments represent what many women feel today.

Most men do not understand that a life devoid of the Spirit of Christ, lacking His grace, is coarse, whereas Spirit-filled righteousness refines character.

Sin desensitizes emotions and concern for others. The Holy Spirit, on the other hand, brings sensitivity to others' needs, hurts, and desires. The very nature of God is to work for the good of others, and that servant's heart is best exhibited in Jesus—the servant Savior for all. The same Spirit who empowered Him works in us to:

- create a servant's heart
- augment our natural talent
- maximize our personality
- highlight our awareness of people's needs and desires
- give insight into life's meaning
- deepen our understanding
- sharpen and clarify issues

This Spirit is a perfect gentleman, granting us the virtues of gentlemanliness, the fruit of the Spirit: "love, joy, peace, patience, kindness, goodness, faithfulness, gentleness and self-control" (Gal. 5:22–23 NIV). The same virtues are also characteristics of ladylikeness, for they are without gender.

By contrast, the "works of the flesh" are sins of uncontrolled sensual passion, superstition, social disorder, and excess (Gal. 5:19–21). All of these scour our mind, soul, and body.

What does all this have to do with marriage? Simply this: God, the ultimate gentleman, is in the business of making gentlemen out of husbands. And more men need to let the Spirit do His work in their lives because the dissolution of many marriages is caused by the absence of gentlemanly qualities among husbands.

How do the characteristics of a gentleman display themselves? In such commonplace things as appearance, manners, speech, hygiene and habits, as well as in character traits.

Many husbands expect their wives to compete with the movie "sex goddesses" physically, while exempting themselves from such comparisons with other men. Although men (or women) don't need to strive for unrealistic images of perfection, men can take great strides toward self-improvement. Failure to take care of physical appearance and attire can cause men to lose respect in women's eyes. Men whose speech is profane, filled with slang and off-color humor, or limited in vocabulary and willful ignorance frequently bar themselves from more intimate relationships. Where good hygiene is possible but neglected, women are repulsed. In short, men who are indifferent to the characteristics of a gentleman diminish their stature, especially to their wives. It is amazing that, in the amount of mail I get from both men and women, such a large percentage of the complaints from women deal with the man's indifference to the common courtesies of life.

"Let each esteem others better than himself" is a biblical bidding for courtesy (Phil. 2:3). If a man reads the Bible for no other reason than to find a blueprint for a gentlemanly life-style, it would be a rich and rewarding experience. Just following the exhortations to courteousness, refinement, and respect for others will lead to gentlemanliness. But let's take a closer look at the fruit of a gentlemanly nature.

Gentleness, one aspect of the fruit of the Spirit, is a sign of true strength in a man, not weakness. When a man knows his strength, he can afford to be gentle. The stronger the man is, the more gentle he can be. Insecure men compensate for their lack by abusing others. Putting someone down doesn't build anyone up. King David, with his powerful war record, great riches, and reputation, wrote of His relationship with God, saying, "Your gentleness has made me great."

Kindness is a virtue that is attractive to women. Men and women were not created as competitors. Women were created to *complete* men. When men make women compete with them for attention, affection, attachment, they defeat themselves and nature. Having "brotherly affection" is to be considerate and sympathetic toward others (Rom. 12:10). This is critical in marriage.

In all fairness to men, I must admit that women seem cut from a different cloth today than in the past. It still astonishes me to hear women speak of men's "cute buns" in an aggressive manner with the crudeness formerly found mostly in men. Femininity is a woman's "stock in trade," her strength of nature, and a glory to her. Why give it up for competitive conflict?

Humility is not weakness (Eph. 4:2, Col. 3:12 KJV). It comes from the Spirit of God. Moses was called the meekest man on earth (Num. 12:3), but he was far from weak. He learned to control his spirit far off in the desert where he was disciplined by God for forty years before beginning his public ministry. And his ministry was to confront and defeat the greatest political figure in his land, then lead about two million Hebrews out of slavery and into the Promised Land. No task for a weak person!

Leadership scares many men. Unfortunately many women must bear the burden of male cowardliness. The unwillingness of men to face the realities of responsibility in marriage literally forces women into a man's role. It is unnatural, but common.

Women have risen to prominence in world leadership today. As in the Church, men have largely abdicated the roles of leadership, forcing women to fill the gap, so in the world today women politicians often enjoy more credibility than the men they have replaced. It is not strange anymore to find top social and political spots in major American cities occupied solely by women.

Houston for years had the reputation of being a "man's town." Texans to the core, Houstonians were proud of their heritage and lineage. Oil men, cattle barons, media moguls, and just plain "good ole boys" gave Houston its male aura. But no more. In Houston, the recently elected woman university president brought the number of women leading that city to six. Other positions occupied by women were the mayor, hospital chief, Chamber of Commerce president, chief of police, and school superintendent.[1]

As men have stepped aside from leadership, and specifically from the leadership of the home, they have found less fulfillment in life. Forty-eight percent of middle managers in major companies in a recent survey said their lives seemed "empty and meaningless," despite the years striving to achieve professional goals. Of senior executives, 68 percent said they had neglected their family in pursuit of professional goals, and that if they could do it over again, they would spend more time with their wives and children. Of high achievers overall, 60 percent felt they had sacrificed their identities to pursue material rewards.[2]

Recognition of others' uniqueness demonstrates strength. Women were created with a God-given uniqueness. When that uniqueness is satisfied, she is that man's wife, best friend, and the completion of his life. When the uniqueness is ignored, stifled, or simply lusted after, she is just another unfulfilled woman.

One woman in exasperation wrote me this letter: "The number one problem in marriage is not lust—it is television. My husband has been involved in church ministry for years, and all our friends have grown in the Lord, but not us. And do you know why? Because he never reads his Bible. He just sits in front of the TV every night while I take care of the children, do the chores, clean the house, and get myself ready for work the next day. I wish it would blow up!"

In a previous book I wrote about the "Video Daddy." The only thing worse than the wimp, brute, or idiot portrayed on the screen is the one glued to it. Television is actually a medium of lust. Programs and commercials are full of it. Not just sexual, but in material goods, food, and that "lust for life." Remember, sex was made for loving and giving, not lusting and getting.

A couple recently told me of the lustful marriage they had lived with for years. Jeff was an entrepreneur by nature, and they had lived in many different cities, working in many businesses through the years. Everywhere they went, Emily worked side by side with him tirelessly, raising the family as well, tending to their various houses, adapting to new communities, and providing him with everything in an attempt to satisfy him.

When the last child finished college, Emily felt herself cool in her relationship to Jeff. She was tired. Nothing she had ever done had been quite good enough. She had never worked to his satisfaction in their businesses. Their marriage bed had never left Jeff completely satisfied. Every time Jeff walked past her, he grabbed at her sexually.

She began to avoid him, became irritable, and kept him at a distance. As the marriage began to dissolve, someone gave Jeff a tape on "Love or Lust." Jeff heard more than what was on the tape; he heard God speaking to him.

Weeks later, as Jeff continued in prayer and soul-searching to hear more from God, he took Emily away for the weekend. In the car, he turned on the tape.

"This is the tape that changed my life," he said.

She laughs now that she expected it to be a trick to get her to listen to a message on woman's submission. Instead, she was shocked to hear a confrontational message of truth that nailed Jeff's every flaw. Before the tape ended, Jeff turned it down, leaned toward Emily and began to ask for forgiveness for thirty years of lusting for her, not loving her. In tears, they made a new commitment to each other and allowed the restoration process to begin.

Not only do men have appetites and desires, but women have

theirs too. Though the needs are often met differently, the basics are the same for both.

According to a recent survey, nearly 50 percent of American wives "cheat" on their husbands by having extramarital affairs. This is double the number in 1948. The reasons the wives gave were:

- to force a change in the relationship
- to "prove" their desirability
- to pursue their dream of a "perfect" love
- to relieve boredom and satisfy curiosity
- to take revenge for the husband's known or suspected infidelity, neglect, stinginess, mistreatment of the children, poor personal hygiene

The underlying cause in every reason given is that the woman's uniqueness was not satisfied in the marriage relationship. Her creativity was stifled. Spontaneity was stunted. Sexual overtures were ignored. Romantic inclinations were thwarted.

Some women simply cannot stand the sight of their husbands around the home on the weekends—unshaven, disheveled, loathsome. One tip written by Abigail Van Buren was: "Don't look like a slob all weekend—unless she looks worse."

It comes back to being a gentleman.

Marriage is the second most important relationship men and women will ever have, and the choice of a mate is the second most important decision they will ever make. The most important is believing on Jesus and building a relationship with God.

The more like Jesus he becomes, the more of a gentleman he will be. Real men are gentlemen. Gentlemen are real men.

Gentlemen make real marriages.

Chapter 22
The Fabulous Father

The legacy of fathers is in their children.

The father is to be the head of the family as Christ is the head of the Church, and he should serve his family in the way Christ serves the Church—as prophet, priest, and king. As prophet, the father speaks from God to his children. As priest, he speaks for his children to God. As king, he governs, qualifying himself to lead by his willingness to serve them. Fathers are to be esteemed and respected, stewards who are greatly rewarded.

There is a problem in fatherhood today, however, which is a direct result of the crisis in manhood. We see men in a spectrum ranging from "Fabulous Fathers" to "Deadly Dads."

America's transition from a producer to a consumer nation brought a marked change in family mind set, which has led in part to the present problems. Young people began to desire to be satisfied, rather than working to satisfy. This helped to bring on the "me generation," where the goal was to satisfy self, which degenerated into the present theology of solipsism, the deifying of self. This philosophy, together with media representation of fathers as a joke, and other profound influences have produced deleterious results that are staggering.

Growing children now are often left to themselves with just television to raise them. "Latchkey" kids, the products of working parents prevalent in America today, easily fall prey to evil from lax discipline and a listless attitude. Television is a thief robbing time, stealing initiative, and killing relationships. Most children spend more hours watching television than they do in school, leaving little time for rightful role models. Australia, a country that attempts to maintain high standards from their media, reported the average preschooler spends thirty hours per week watching television. Students spent more than 15,000 hours watching television during school years, while receiving 11,000 hours of education. For every seven hours spent watching television, children spent only one hour reading.[1] One cause of widespread low student test scores is said to be poor stewardship of children's time, as television steals more and more of their day.

No wonder teens are in trouble. William Bennett is the former Secretary of Education for the United States. He voiced this concern:

> Never before has one generation of American teenagers been less healthy, less cared for, or less prepared for life than their parents were at the same age. Many—perhaps most—of the problems that worry us are not rooted in institutional bigotry, governmental neglect, societal hardheartedness or disease, but in behavior. And their solutions depend on our willingness to reassert the moral and ethical values of family, community, and character.
>
> Government never raised a child, and it never will. Nothing more powerfully determines a child's behavior than his internal compass, his beliefs, his sense of right and wrong. The character of a society is determined this way; by means of individual morality accruing social capital from generation to generation.[2]

Judge Moore, a Los Angeles juvenile court judge said,

> Young people today woefully lack the basic skills of reading, writing, arithmetic. They are illiterates, not because they are ignorant, but because they are educationally handicapped. They are not properly taught, motivated or guided. I have long advocated adding a parenting class to the school curriculum and making it a mandatory requirement for graduation from junior high school and high school.[3]

Speaking from his profession, he quoted a horrible finding: "It is a proven fact that 85 to 90 percent of all delinquent children have been abused, either sexually, emotionally, or physically."[4]

When parenting has provided only provocation, crooked strokes, or abuse, a poor self-image is the result. Valueless to self, life itself is worthless, so what point is there in living? For those who don't find worth by immoral, illicit, or illegal means, suicide becomes an option. Suicide is the second leading cause of death among America's youth.

Those who survive teen years are now caught in the backwash of the "baby boom," whose culture and attitudes still dominate American discourse. This "baby bust" generation, in the eighteen-to-twenty-nine bracket, seem almost to be rebelling against rebellion. Apathy and alienation are giving way to disengagement. The findings of two national studies paint a portrait of a generation of these young adults as people indifferent toward public affairs. One reports,

> It is a generation that knows less, cares less, votes less, and is less critical of its leaders and institutions than young people in the past. . . . It is not so much that young adults under thirty are disillusioned, as they are uninterested.[5]

Another study concludes that there is a "citizenship crisis" in which "America's youth are alarmingly ill-prepared to keep democracy alive in the 1990s and beyond."[6]

The greatest mission for men today is not to correct what is wrong in adults, but to reach and teach what is right to children and youth.

Where values and goals are not taught in the home, and where educational processes deny responsibility for teaching moral values, where will young men and women find them? We must not be deceived into thinking that institutions, philosophically adulterated authority figures, or media-made role models will teach our children the principles upon which to build not only their lives, but those of their family and nation. The home is the place where these are to be inculcated into the life. The person ultimately responsible is the father. For those without fathers, a fatherly role model from friend or neighbor is vital to sons of single mothers.

Young men must be mentored in the ways of morality, goodness, and righteousness. For men who have found the answer to the world's problems through Christ, their efforts need to be focused on becoming mentors to the young. Men cannot allow the wisdom, experience, and knowledge to die with them. They *must* invest those spiritual, physical, and material resources God has entrusted to them and make every effort to incorporate them into the lives of the young. Teen-men need to know what real manhood is. They will not find it except in men like you reading this right now.

During the days of the "hippie" generation, when revolutionary-minded students beleaguered and besieged California colleges, when drugs were openly advocated, and some professors told collegians to "tune in, turn on, and drop out," I served on Governor Reagan's "Council on Children and Youth." Among our responsibilities was to do a survey of rehabilitation units in the state to analyze their effectiveness, discover who had the lowest rate of recidivism, and why. At the time it was startling to discover that the most successful rehab centers were those that were closest to approximating family life. The closer they could come to a "surrogate family" the more successful they became. Teen Challenge had the lowest rate of recidivism among those we surveyed.

"Family" means "father's house." Father's problems are sown as seeds into children and reaped as adults. Psychologists attempt to delve into a patient's childhood (especially the first seven years) and the family tree to try to find the roots of problems.

In a survey published in a national news service, there were four basic causes listed as to why children become vulnerable and susceptible to drugs and alcohol. They are: low ambition level, poor self-image, low sociability, and emotional deprivation. These factors become critical warning signs that an otherwise normal child is becoming liable to abnormal habits or associations.

A father's responsibility in the home is to provide intimacy, discipline, love, and worth. To the neglected, abused, and excluded, cults offer what the home failed to provide: intimacy, discipline, love, and worth. Cults thrive on disenfranchised and alienated youths. Interestingly, the same four qualities were provided in the most successful rehab centers surveyed: intimacy, discipline, love, and worth.

Bob Larson in his masterful treatise about cults states: they "demote God, devalue Christ, deify man, and denigrate Scripture."[7] What they do offer is family relationships that the young respond to. Having missed it at home, the cult becomes the substitute family, and the leader or guru a father figure.

Mr. Larson says to combat cults, fathers must teach children:

- the attributes of God,
- person of Christ,
- nature of man,

- requirements of salvation,
- and the source of all true revelation.[8]

These "tenets of faith" cannot be left to some Sunday school teacher, children's church worker, itinerant preacher, or pastor. It is the work of ministry in the father who is prophet, priest, and king in his own home. These tenets are not commonly taught in the home today, as they were in previous generations, because men in the average congregation are untutored in the doctrines themselves, and thus cannot pass them along to their children. Men can only pass on to their children what they possess.

There was a day in history when fathers in the home were the teachers, and books were the center of family life. Reading to the family in the evening brought culture, attentiveness, quietness, and knowledge. It created an image of the father's authority in the family's mind. It was not uncommon that fathers did not have to discipline, but merely speak and children obeyed. If children do not learn the work ethic at home, nor how to set and attain short- and long-term goals, aspiration to achieve in the individual life will typically be underdeveloped, if not lost altogether.

We are stewards, not owners, of our children. A man's stewardship can never be relinquished, and judgment of him comes from the measure to which he succeeds. A father can be both a "Deadly Dad" and a "Fabulous Father," both in one home to two different children.

King David was a deadly dad to his son Adonijah, but a fabulous father to Solomon. The Bible records that "his father, King David, had never disciplined him [Adonijah] at any time—not so much as by a single scolding" (1 Kings 1:6 LB). Lack of correction from his father ruined Adonijah. It is an accepted fact that the quickest way to destroy a child is to give a child anything he wants.

When Solomon was to inherit the throne of his father, David prepared for the transition by giving his wealth to Solomon to carry out the construction of the Temple and exhorted Solomon he would need to be wise, planting the seed in Solomon's heart that became the basis for requesting wisdom from God.

Adonijah rebelled against his father, but Solomon submitted. Sibling rivalries often have their roots in parental upbringing. Jacob loved Joseph more than his other sons, gifted him with a coat of many colors, and created the hostility and jealousy that turned to hatred in the hearts of Joseph's brothers.

Deadly dads can be doting dads, drinking dads, discordant dads, demanding dads, dividing dads, demeaning dads, defeated dads, departed dads, or even demonic dads.

Fabulous fathers, on the other hand, want to see their sons and daughters grow to maturity, be productive, develop normally, and enjoy their own families. A man cannot expect to become a "Fabulous Father" by chance. Like anything, good fathering takes study, practice, and time. I cannot attempt to cover every fathering skill in one chapter. Good books on the subject abound. But I can give these highlights to get you started.

Normal adolescence can be divided into three stages, says Dr. Robert L. Hendren, head of the American Academy of Child Psychiatry's committee on adolescence. Some typical ways they behave during their turbulent and tumultuous teens are:

Early adolescence (12–14 years):

- Begin questioning parents' values
- Often moody
- Form closer friendships; would rather go out with their friends than with their parents
- Realize parents aren't perfect; identify their faults
- Follow interests and clothing styles of peer groups

Middle adolescence (14–17 years):

- Become self-involved, alternating between unrealistically high expectations and poor self-concept
- Complain that parents interfere with independence
- Extremely concerned with appearance and with their bodies; start primping and strutting their stuff
- Have a lower opinion of parents, withdraw emotionally from them, and form sense of identity from peer group

Late adolescence (17–19 years):

- Form firmer identity; have a better sense of who they are and what they stand for
- Become better at expressing feelings with words
- More developed sense of humor

- More emotionally stable; don't have the wide mood swings of previous stages
- Take more pride in their work; more self-reliant[9]

The wise father will take note of what motivates his child through these years and work to channel the energy, not stifle creativity.

God requires fathers: "Do not provoke your children to wrath, but bring them up in the training and admonition of the Lord" (Eph. 6:4).

The apostle John wrote, "I have no greater joy than to hear that my children walk in truth" (3 John 4). A father's primary purpose in parenting is the eternal welfare of his family. It is his responsibility to train his children to live on their own foundation of faith, character, and experience, raise them in the nurture and admonition of the Lord, not to provoke them to wrath, and to teach them God's ways so they in turn can teach their own children.

Fathers provide teaching and training of righteousness within the home. This includes teaching the sexual sign of the covenant God gives to married people. It is the father's honor to present his children as virgins on the day of their weddings. Teaching a child about his or her sexuality is occurring earlier and earlier because of the vast amounts of sexual aberrations our society exposes to children. Teaching them at least in part before the onset of puberty is critical.

Fathers are to guard against defilement. Physically fathers guard children from abuse, abortion, and addiction. Mentally, fathers guard children from evil reports of all kinds—gossip, films, harshly critical teachers. Spiritually, fathers guard against the attacks of the enemy, including discouragement and depression.

Godly fathers need to love as God loves: redemptively, sacrificially, and unconditionally. In this same manner a husband is to love his wife as Christ loves the church.

As God loves us, fathers must love their families. A father needs to give his children something that cannot be bought: himself. Toys, no matter how sophisticated, do not replace the person. Nothing impersonal can satisfy the personal. A fabulous father must give his children acceptance, approval, affection, association, and a sense of authority.

A young woman wrote me a letter filled with pathos encouraging me to continue to minister to men. The reason, she wrote, was that she was born with a physical impediment and because of it her father never accepted her. Rejection was all she knew until she found the acceptance of her heavenly Father through Jesus Christ. That saved her life.

A sense of association comes from a well-developed sense of belonging. Fathers must make their children feel as though they belong to the family. This is especially true of stepfathers. It's too easy for stepdads to favor their own natural children and withhold the same approval, affection, and association with the stepchildren. I already told the story of the man who was faithful to his own children, but not to his stepchildren. As a result, he was experiencing poor behavior from his own children and the stepchildren.

Acceptance, approval, affection, association, and a sense of authority make a strong foundation. What is built on that foundation is even more directly the father's responsibility because the healthy child watches and copies his dad. Children learn by example. It is not the father's responsibility to make all his children's decisions for them, but to let them see him make his.

Children may not always listen to you, but they will always imitate you.

This father wrote to me when he found that out:

> One statement that you made, "The character of the kingdom emanates from the character of the king," helped me change as a father. My eldest son, Zachary, nine years old, had been asking me to draw pictures of jet planes for him. He is fascinated by them, likes to read books about them, and likes jet toys. Every time he would ask me to draw for him I would tell him, "I don't know how, and besides it's too hard." This sequence happened repeatedly, with me answering the same way each time.
>
> A few months later we received a note from his teacher saying that Zachary was not turning in his homework assignments. My wife and I checked his assignments and told him to make sure he turned them in. A few weeks later we received another note that said he had improved, but still was not turning in his homework. I discovered he had done his homework but didn't turn it in. I told him he couldn't play until he turned in his work and asked his teacher to give him make-up work. Again he didn't turn it in. This time I disciplined him and requested a parent-teacher conference, hoping that God would show me through the conference what the problem was with my son.

I asked the teacher what might be the reason for his behavior. My heart dropped when she said he repeatedly told her, "It's too hard, and besides I don't know how."

I remembered another thing you said once, "You'll never beat out of your child what is wrong in your own life." Change had to come first in my own life—so that change could happen in my son. I immediately began to draw those jet planes, and my son slowly began to do his homework.

Starting with changing yourself, you can change a multitude of lives around you too. Be a fabulous father to your children and the fatherless around you. Accept the mission to teach children and teen-men what you have spent a lifetime learning.

Don't bury your legacy of faith when you die. Plant it in some young mind and heart, and let it live long after you're gone. Every son needs a father; every young man needs a mentor. Deadly dad or fabulous father—you make the choice.

Chapter 23
The Authentic Friend

I found Brad in his motel room. After our initial brotherly greeting and embrace, we settled into chairs and he began repeating, "It's been unbelievable."

Years before, Brad stood to make his commitment to Christ in one of our events. He became a friend, helped support the ministry, and he and his wife became friends with our staff. Now alone, in the midst of a divorce, far from his home, he and I sat in the privacy of his motel room, and I listened to his tearfully told story.

Brad had a trusted partner who carried on his business on a daily basis. But this erstwhile dependable individual did something Brad considered immoral and seditious. When confronted by Brad, he refused to acknowledge wrong, rebelled, and had to be fired.

The fired partner then went to work for someone else, took most of Brad's business with him, and left Brad mentally confused, emotionally crushed, and spiritually debilitated. When the pressure of it reached into Brad's home, his wife did not respond as he thought she should. Overwhelmed, he "opted out." His wife later verified that she had been selfishly disposed, didn't support him, and now wished she could do it all over. Weeping as she spoke of her departed husband, she pleaded, "Please, Ed, do what you can."

There was little I could do in that lonely motel room. The best thing to do, I thought, was pray with him and be his friend. I put my hand on his shoulder and said, "Brad, I want to be a friend and help you all I can."

Instead of accepting my gesture, he looked up at me sharply and said, "I've heard that before!" He paused then asked, "What is a friend? Does anyone know how to be a friend? The men I trusted said they were my friends, but they weren't." His remarks left a sick sense in my gut, like a ten-ton sledge hammer had hit me.

Faithful friends are life's greatest treasure. The unfaithful, as Brad discovered, are life's greatest hurt. Being a true friend is one of the marks of a real man.

Brad's former partner was a traitor. Traitors are not friends, regardless of their professed friendship. In a recent nonfiction book, the author tells of his training as a spy. One experienced spy told him, "Always remember the most important thing: When I am sitting with my friend, he is not sitting with his friend."[1] There is a vast difference between the men's regard for each other. One is trusting, the other trusts no one. The author explained that, to spies, traitors are the lowest of the low. Yet, he said, "Every agent [spy] is a traitor, no matter how much he rationalizes it."[2] He is a traitor and not a true friend.

Judas is regarded with contempt more than pity because he betrayed Jesus. Trusted with the treasury, Judas forgot he was only a steward and not the owner of what he possessed. For the love of money Judas turned traitor and died a most ignominious death.

A man is also not a friend if he advises devious deeds that will lead to ruin. In the biblical story of Amnon and Tamar it is clear that were it not for a "friend" who devised Amnon's rape of Tamar, neither of their lives would have been ruined. Jonadab, who gave Amnon the plan, was no friend (2 Sam. 13). If Jonadab had been a true friend he would have warned Amnon of the course he was taking to prevent such actions, rather than advocating and advancing the scheme that would be a personal disaster.

King David was suffering from being betrayed by his most trusted friend when he wrote,

> Even my own familiar friend in whom I trusted,
> Who ate my bread,
> Has lifted up his heel against me. (Ps. 41:9)

David's words prophetically applied to our Lord Jesus when he was betrayed by Judas. Yet Jesus cried on the cross, "Father, forgive them, for they do not know what they do" (Luke 23:34). He forgave every offense.

When we are wounded, hurt, or offended by those we regard as friends, those we trust, we cannot allow their feigned faith, hypocrisy, or misdeeds to cause us to become bitter and turn against the Lord who is our only hope. We must die to those things by giving them to the Lord in prayer—trusting Him who already bore it all to heal and sustain us in our trial.

Why walk away from a friend who loved us enough to die in our stead that we might have eternal life? Only a fool would do that! If we turn away from Jesus and toward the "weak and beggarly elements" of the world (Gal. 4:9) to give us comfort or assuage our hurts, we receive only superficial solace and become worse off than ever. What comfort is there in alcohol or drink? It only deceives us and becomes our master while promising to serve us by giving relief. What ease is there from television with its philosophical perversion propagating immorality that only temporarily salves our bitterness while deepening feelings of anarchy against God? Or the "friendly" woman who provides the "sympathetic shoulder" and open bed, but who only creates more distress when she proves as unfaithful again as she did to the man she left? There is no healing—only more betrayal and hurt, greater hardening of heart—and what seems good turns out to be evil.

Jesus is our only refuge! The Bible says, "Do not cast away your confidence, which has great reward" (Heb. 10:35). Jesus Himself told us that in this world we would have tribulation, but to "be of good cheer, I have overcome the world" (John 16:33). Peter added that, though the saints' faith would be "tested by fire, may [it] be found to praise, honor, and glory at the revelation of Jesus Christ" (1 Peter 1:7).

When I left Brad's room that evening, my next appointment was a meeting with leaders of our Southern California "Maximized Manhood" rallies. Still hurting in my heart because of my friend's despair, I asked those leaders, "What is a friend to you?" Their replies were:

- "A friend is someone who knows all my faults and accepts me just as I am."
- "A friend is someone who loves me enough to speak into my life and tell me the truth I need to hear."
- "A friend is someone with whom I can be transparent, vulnerable, and honest."
- "The measure of a friend is the degree to which I can share my life with him and not have it come back to me."
- "A friend is someone I can count on in a crisis."
- "A friend to me is like what Jonathan and David had in the Bible."
- "A friend will not leave me or forsake me."

I guess I shouldn't have been surprised to see that each answer described Jesus! Jesus truly is "a friend who sticks closer than a brother" (Prov. 18:24). Friendship with Jesus is our greatest hope in times of trouble!

Requirements to be a true friend are greater than to be an acquaintance. Jesus fulfills every one. He said; "No longer do I call you servants . . . but I have called you friends" (John 15:15). Scripture says, "Faithful are the wounds of a friend" (Prov. 27:6); "A friend loves at all times" (Prov. 17:17); "Greater love has no one than this, than to lay down one's life for his friends" (John 15:13).

We learn how to be friends by studying the friendship of Jesus. True friends are loyal, trustworthy, true, and steadfast. Friends help in times of crisis and the crisis deepens the friendship. The strongest friendships are those forged in the furnace of affliction. To set aside your own concerns in an attempt to resolve another's crisis is a form of dying to yourself. When it's true friendship, it is done unselfishly with love and devotion.

When King David was faced with the sedition of Absalom, his son, and the defection by his trusted advisor Ahithophel, David prayed that God would confound the counsel of Ahithophel. God sent another friend, Hushai, to meet David's need. In a time of crisis it was the loyalty of a real friend that enabled David to regain his throne (2 Sam. 15:30–37). Hushai laid down his life for David and found a firmer friendship with the king. Ahithophel tried to save his life and eventually lost it (2 Sam. 16—17).

True friends rejoice when their friends do well. Taking joy in another's success provides real fulfillment.

My wife is my best friend. She takes great joy in my success and is the greatest contributor to it. A wife who is a real friend to her husband is a man's greatest protection and source of inspiration and solace. Nancy knows everything about me. When we learned the nine principles of intercession, it changed my life. During prayer times together I became open and vulnerable, able to share my weaknesses with her, knowing she would pray for me—not condemn me. Our relationship was strengthened through the trust developed in friendship.

A wife who is not a real friend has little to offer. Job's wife, in her bitterness caused by resentment at her loss, told her husband to "curse God and die" (Job 2:9). She was no help in his distress. Neither were the friends who came to mourn and comfort him, only to become an object lesson of what not to be. Friends are those who speak truth into your life in a time of need, but these men spoke from self-righteous prejudices and not from God's perspective. To make a friend, you must first be friendly (Prov. 18:24).

Friends are life's greatest treasure. It is friendship, not romance, that holds a marriage together. Affection between friends can be even stronger than love between husband and wife. Jonathan and David had that type of friendship, and Scripture describes it as that "surpassing the love of women" (2 Sam. 1:26).

Life's greatest commodity is not money but friends. Businessmen need to learn to make friends, not customers. When the clients and customers are all gone in times of recession and depression, friends will still be doing business. Friend-raising rather than fundraising is the key to longevity in business because "funds come from friends."

Abraham "was called the friend of God" (James 2:23). What greater appellation or accolade can be accorded any man than to have God call him a "friend." God spoke to Moses "face to face, as a man speaks to his friend" (Exod. 33:11).

What could be greater than having God call you His friend? Real men need to learn to be friends, with other men, with their wives and children, and also with Jesus Christ by accepting the friendship He clearly offers.

Chapter 24

The Greatest Pleasure in Life

Nancy and I like to take trips together to minister in England. We love the British: their sense of humor, Wimbledon, and their tea. On a recent trip there, I read an article by an Englishman who was complaining about how his countrymen apologize for success. He said *success* was almost a dirty word in their culture and that great achievements are often followed by an apology for having done so well. The writer traced the attitude to the ancient Greeks. According to him, their philosophy was "Don't get too bumptious, lest you make the gods jealous and they strike you down."

He closed his article with this:

> I'd like to see us shuck off those ancient Greeks and try another God. One who is never jealous, who wants a world where everyone can win at something, who sets high standards but forgives mistakes; a culture where celebration is okay, where joy is part of life and Heaven is still ahead. Of course, it would be quite a revolution.[1]

In the Christian community we could be given the same ribbing. So often we act like we're trying to keep from riling God, trying to pacify Him with good works without sharing in the joy of having done them. Scripture states, however, that God *is* pleased with us. If we accept and understand that, we approach life eagerly, expecting to please Him and freely expressing the joy it brings. There is an exuberance, a sense of excitement when a man pleases God, that nothing else can produce. There is no need for guilt, embarrassment, or shame in attempting to please Him. And there is no mystery in learning how to please Him.

We were in Washington, D.C., at a Christian Men's Event on a day that seemed to be a throwback to the old, great church revivals. The Holy Spirit would sweep over entire auditoriums during those days, calling men to repentance and displaying the glory of the risen Savior. On this particular June day, we could almost see God's "Glory Cloud" descend as men ran to the altar to throw their lives to God with abandon, deeply repenting for anything unclean. Like that day I recounted in Boston, men began to throw on the stage whatever they considered to be a proof of their former lives now being abandoned in favor of a new life in Christ. It was powerful, emotionally draining, spiritually edifying, physically sanctifying, mentally illuminating, and glorifying to God.

Vietnam veterans' hearts and minds that had suffered the nightmares, bitterness, envy, enmity, and hatred were cleansed by the Word and the Spirit of Jesus Christ. Former adulterers openly declared their purification from lustful thoughts and desires. Husbands declared new love for their wives. They were moved to be the men God created them to be and the husbands their wives desired them to be. What a glorious few hours we had together!

God was so pleased with the repentance, faith, honesty, openness, truthfulness, and reality the men were exhibiting that He freely poured out blessing upon blessing. Men experienced the primitive power of God working deep within them and one after another stood to tell what God had done.

Pleasing God brought His favor, blessing, power, and joy.

People spend hundreds, thousands, millions of dollars on drugs and alcohol to get Satan's counterfeit of the uninhibited joy and celebration of being a man. Doctors, lawyers, and psychologists are at this very moment receiving monies from people who hope to obtain what God so freely gives.

Christians who contemplate how man displeases God often become blind to the Scriptures that aptly describe how well we really please Him. I read a letter from a minister last week about the "last days" and how God was going to judge the world. Yes, there is a place for that understanding. But let's not let the negative outweigh the positive message that men can give God pleasure!

There are times I don't please God; times I don't even please myself, and especially others. But I press on, and on and on, knowing that with my increasing obedience there are more times He is pleased than when He is displeased.

The Bible counsels us to "have a walk worthy of the Lord, fully pleasing Him" (Col. 1:10); God accomplishes the "good pleasure of His will" (Eph. 1:5) in us; and, "God works in you both to will and to do for His good pleasure" (Phil. 2:13). God does the work in us so He can be pleased with us.

To walk in God's will for our lives, as real men, secure in our manhood and our relationship with Him, is our highest good. Our highest good gives God pleasure.

When we please God, we are working for our own highest good.

Jesus said, "Do not fear, little flock, for it is your Father's good pleasure to give you the kingdom" (Luke 12:32).

God is working both to give and produce the kingdom of God in us. That is where His pleasure is. God has no pleasure in wickedness (Ps. 5:4), nor the death of the wicked (Ezek. 18:23, 33:11), and no pleasure in fools. Those in the flesh cannot please God, neither can those without faith in Him (Rom. 8:8; Heb. 11:6).

Jesus said, "I do always those things that please Him" (John 8:29). Jesus had the testimony that "He pleased God." God the Father even told the world, "This is My beloved Son, in whom I am well pleased" (Matt. 3:17).

God was not just pleased in Jesus as deity, but God was pleased in the very manhood that Jesus Christ displayed. We, like Jesus, give God pleasure when we

- have faith in His Son (Heb. 11:6)
- obey Him (1 John 3:22)
- are led by His Spirit (Rom. 8:14)
- praise Him (Ps. 69:30–31)
- serve Him (John 12:26)
- give to His ministry (2 Cor. 9:7)

God takes pleasure in those who fear Him. God has pleasure in His people (Ps. 149:4). He is pleased when we make ourselves look foolish by sharing His gospel with others so they can be saved (1 Cor. 1:21).

Even when we sin and bring guilt and condemnation in our life, it is still possible to please God by our repentance (Ps. 51:19).

Pleasing God has the greatest benefit in the world (heaven), gives the greatest satisfaction in life (reality), and achieves the greatest accomplishment in life (Christlikeness).

Whatever you have done or tried to be in life, however you have succeeded or failed, to what degree of manhood you have attained or come short, now is the time to make a quality decision to become a "real man."

This is the place, you are the man, Christ is the Lord, and this is the time to pray this prayer with me—mean it— and allow the Holy Spirit to begin a new work in your life at this moment.

Dear God,
I am a man. I want to be a real man, so those things in my life that are wrong, where I have made mistakes, committed my errors and sins, forgive me. I want them out of my life. Right now I ask you to come into my life by Your Spirit and change me. Make me to be the man you created me to be through Jesus Christ. Thank You, Lord. Amen.

Thank God you're a man.
Thank God you're real.
Be a real man!

NOTES

CHAPTER 1 THE MASCULINITY CRISIS

1. David Nyhan, "Wanted: Some Stouthearted Men," *Boston Sunday Globe*, 7 May 1988, 87.
2. Jim Felton, "Soviets Can't Forget Horrors of World War II," *Daily Pilot*, 20 Sept. 1989, 12.
3. Edwin Louis Cole, *The Potential Principle* (Pittsburgh: Whitaker House, 1984).

CHAPTER 2 THE SUBSTITUTE SOCIETY

1. Bill Murray, *Values Clarification and the Christian* (Dallas: MFM Publishing, 1983), citing Richard A. Baer, "Parents, Schools, and Values Clarification," *Wall Street Journal*, 12 April 1982, 22.
2. Nicols Fox, "What Are Our Real Values?" *Newsweek*, 13 Feb. 1989, 8.
3. William Murchison, "Protestant Ethic Is Needed," *Dallas Morning News*, 23 Sept. 1989.
4. "Young Britain: A Survey of Youth Culture in Transition" by Euromonitor and Carrick James Market Research, London, 1987–1988.
5. Tim Robertson, *Pat Robertson's Perspective* (Virginia Beach, VA: CBN, 1987).
6. Paul Johnson, *Intellectuals* (New York: Harper and Row, 1988), 64–65.
7. Ibid, 23.
8. Mortimer B. Zuckerman, "Old Liberalism, New Politics," *U.S. News & World Report*, 7 Nov. 1988, 99.
9. State of Rhode Island and Providence Plantations, Division of Taxation, Final Decision and Order, 28 July 1989.

CHAPTER 3 CRACKS IN THE MIRROR

1. Thomas C. Reeves, *A Question of Character* (Glencoe: Free Press, 1991).
2. Lee Colodny and Robert Gettlin, *Silent Coup* (New York: St. Martin's Press, 1991).
3. Austin Murphy, "A Lamb Among Lions," *Sports Illustrated*, 10 Sept. 1990, 61–64.

CHAPTER 5 JESUS: THE PATTERN OF LIFE

1. Sam Keen and Ofer Zur, "Who Is the New Ideal Man?" *Psychology Today*, Nov. 1989, 58.

CHAPTER 6 JESUS: THE POWER OF LIFE

1. Edwin Louis Cole, *When Life Is Just Too Tough* (Tulsa: Harrison House, 1988).

CHAPTER 7 LIFE-CHANGING VALUES

1. John O. Anderson, *Cry of the Innocents* (South Plainfield, NJ: Bridge Publishing, IN, 1984), 41.
2. John O. Anderson, "Give Us Fathers," *CRY Ministry Newsletter,* 17 Aug. 1991, excerpt of Anderson's unpublished book, *Cry of Compassion.*
3. Michael Hirsley, "Giving Attitudes Are Giving Way," *Chicago Tribune,* 12 Oct. 1990, sec. 2, 8.
4. David Barton, *America: To Pray or Not to Pray* (Aledo, TX: Wall Builder Press, 1991), 10, 41, 68, 75.

CHAPTER 8 MAXIMIZING YOUR RESOURCES

1. "Besieged Dinka Emphasize Physical, Social Stature," *Dallas Morning News,* 11 Sept. 1989.
2. David D. Gilmore, "Manhood," *Natural History,* June 1990, 6–10.
3. David D. Gilmore as quoted by Russel Segal in "It's a World's Man," *Men's Health,* Dec. 1990, 46.
4. David D. Gilmore, *Masculinity in the Making: Cultural Concepts of Masculinity* (New Haven, CT: Yale University Press, 1990).
5. *World Almanac 1991* (New York: Scripps Howard Co., 1991), 467.

CHAPTER 9 STAYING ON TOP

1. George Gallup, Jr., "Commentary on the State of Religion in the U.S. Today," *Gallup Poll,* 1984.
2. Leonard LeSourd, *Strong Men/Weak Men* (Old Tappan, NJ: Chosen Books, 1990), 159.

CHAPTER 11 NOTHING BUT THE TRUTH

1. "Lying, Cheating, Stealing: Ethics in Modern America," *ABC News,* 1 June 1989.
2. Garry Abrams, "Did We Rear a Bunch of 'Moral Mutants'?" *Los Angeles Times,* 11 Oct. 1990, E1, 7–8.
3. Jim Wright, "What Has Become of Trust?" *Dallas Morning News,* 26 Sept. 1989.
4. James C. Dobson, *Love Must Be Tough* (Waco, TX: Word Books, 1983), 44.

CHAPTER 12 LOVE OR LUST

1. Marco R. della Cava, "Sexual Addiction Can Lead to Destruction," *USA Today,* 2 Feb. 1989, 5D.
2. James Dobson, *Focus on the Family,* March 1990.
3. David Jackson, "Minister Pleads Guilty to Rapes," *Dallas Morning News,* 25 Aug. 1989, 33A, 36A.
4. U.S. Department of Justice, Office of Juvenile Justice and Delinquency Prevention, Principal Investigator Judith A. Reisman, Ph.D., "Executive Summary: Images of Children, Crime and Violence in Playboy, Penthouse and Hustler Magazines," Nov. 1987).

5. "Peep Shows Incite Man to Rape," *Christian Voice Washington Report,* July 1984.
6. U.S. Department of Justice, Office of Juvenile Justice and Delinquency Prevention, Principal Investigator Judith A. Reisman, Ph.D., "Executive Summary: Images of Children, Crime and Violence in Playboy, Penthouse and Hustler Magazines," Nov. 1987, 3.
7. George Flesh, "Why I Quit Doing Abortions," *Los Angeles Times,* 12 Sept. 1991, B11.
8. George Grant, *Grand Illusions: The Legacy of Planned Parenthood* (Brentwood, TN: Wolgemuth and Hyatt Publishers, Inc., 1988), 61.

CHAPTER 15   THE WINNING STRATEGY

1. Edwin Louis Cole, *Courage* (Tulsa: Harrison House, 1985).
2. Edwin Louis Cole, *The Potential Principle* (Pittsburgh: Whitaker House, 1984), 14.

CHAPTER 16   EMPLOYED FOR LIFE

1. Morris Cerullo, *Proof Producers* (San Diego: Morris Cerullo World Evangelism, 1979), 25.

CHAPTER 17   FINANCIAL FREEDOM

1. Edwin Louis Cole, *The Potential Principle* (Pittsburgh: Whitaker House, 1984).

CHAPTER 18   POSITIVE STRESS

1. "Research Recommendations," issued by National Institute of Business Management, 6 March 1989, 2.
2. Ian Ball, "Now They Say TV Isn't Even Relaxing," *The [London] Times,* July 1990, citing Dr. Robert Kubey and Dr. Mihaly Csikszentmihalyi, *Television and the Quality of Life: How Viewing Shapes Everyday Experience* (Hillsdale, NJ: Erlbaum, Lawrence, and Associates, Inc., 1990).
3. Ian Ball, "Now They Say TV Isn't Even Relaxing," citing David Frost.
4. Fred Williams, "Office Stress Follows Many Home," *USA Today,* 15 March 1990, 8B, citing survey by Dunhill Personnel System, Inc.
5. "Study Finds a Paying Job Helps Women Beat the Blues," *Orange County Register,* 5 Sept. 1990, K2, citing study by R. Jay Turner, sociology professor at University of Toronto.
6. Dr. T. Berry Brazelton, "Working Parents," *Newsweek,* 13 Feb. 1989, 66–70.
7. Edwin Louis Cole, *When Life Is Just Too Tough* (Tulsa: Harrison House, 1988).

CHAPTER 19   PEACE FOR ALL SEASONS

1. Marlin Maddoux, *The Selling of Gorbachev* (Dallas: International Christian Media, 1988), 65–66.
2. James Reston, "Down Below the Summits, Millions of War Deaths," *The New York Times,* 3 June 1988, I-31.

CHAPTER 20 LEADERSHIP THAT WORKS

1. Mike McKinley, "Secretary of the Navy Challenges Navy's Leaders," *All Hands,* Feb. 1988, 14–15.

CHAPTER 21 THE IRRESISTIBLE HUSBAND

1. Kay Ray, "In Houston, Women Lead," *USA Today,* 2 July 1990, 2.
2. Jan Halper, "Male Mystique," *American Way Magazine,* 1 August 1989, 42–48.

CHAPTER 22 THE FABULOUS FATHERS

1. Australia Children's Television Foundation.
2. William Raspberry, "Kids Need a Moral Compass to Go Straight," *Los Angeles Times,* 26 Oct. 1990.
3. Judge Moore, Los Angeles, CA. Personal quotation. Reprinted by permission.
4. Ibid.
5. Michael Oreskes, "U.S. Youth in the '90s: The Indifferent Generation," *Washington Post,* citing The Times Mirror Center for the People and Press Report and People for the American Way, *New York Times,* 28 June 1990, A1.
6. Ibid.
7. Bob Larson, *Larson's Book of Cults* (Wheaton, IL: Tyndale House Publishers, 1982), 32.
8. Ibid.
9. Dr. Robert L. Hendren, "Those Adolescent Years Are a Turbulent Period," *USA Today.*

CHAPTER 23 THE AUTHENTIC FRIEND

1. Victor Ostrovsky and Claire Hoy, *By Way of Deception: Making and Unmaking of a Mossad Officer* (New York: St. Martin's Press, 1990), 86.
2. Ibid, 98.

CHAPTER 24 THE GREATEST PLEASURE IN LIFE

1. Charles Handy, "Thought for the Day," London, 17 Dec. 1986.

ABOUT THE AUTHOR

Edwin Louis Cole, founder and president of the Christian Men's Network, speaks with a prophetic voice to the men of this generation. His message that "Manhood and Christlikeness are synonymous" declares a standard for manhood that has changed hundreds of thousands of lives. He is an internationally acclaimed speaker, television personality, bestselling author, and motivational lecturer. Cole travels extensively, showing men how to realize their dreams of real manhood by looking to Jesus Christ as their role model.